A Brief History of
Feminism

A Brief History of
Feminism

PATU / ANTJE SCHRUPP

translated by Sophie Lewis

The MIT Press / Cambridge, Massachusetts / London, England

Originally published as *Kleine Geschichte des Feminismus im euro-amerikanischen Kontext*, © UNRAST-Verlag, Münster

This book was set in Myriad Pro and Adobe Garamond Pro by The MIT Press. Printed and bound in the United States of America.

Library of Congress Cataloging-in-Publication Data

Names: Schrupp, Antje, 1964- author. | Patu, (Illustrator)
Title: A brief history of feminism / Patu and Antje Schrupp ; translated by Sophie Lewis.
Other titles: Kleine Geschichte des Feminismus. English
Description: Cambridge, MA : MIT Press, [2017]
Identifiers: LCCN 2017008083 | ISBN 9780262037112 (hardcover : alk. paper)
Subjects: LCSH: Feminism--History.
Classification: LCC HQ1121 .S3313 2017 | DDC 305.4209--dc23 LC record available at https://lccn.loc.gov/2017008083

10 9 8 7 6 5 4 3 2 1

EVE AND ADAM, OR WHAT IS FEMINISM ANYWAY?

Practically every culture claims a fundamental difference between human genders or sexes. Usually, though not always, it's a question of just two: male and female. The principle of two sexes was elaborated in the Bible's account of creation, the story of Adam and Eve.

> And the Lord God caused a deep sleep to fall upon Adam, and he slept: and he took one of his ribs, and closed up the flesh instead thereof; And the rib, which the Lord God had taken from man, made he a woman, and brought her unto the man. And Adam said, This is now bone of my bones, and flesh of my flesh: she shall be called Woman, because she was taken out of Man.

This is often interpreted today to mean that man was created first, and then woman, "from his rib." But actually, the Hebrew word "Adam" is not the name of a man; it is simply the word for "human being." Adam had no gender in the very beginning. The creation of Eve, then, did not so much introduce woman into the world as gender difference. Out of the gender-neutral human being "Adam" came man and woman.

Equating Adam with man already shows us the root of the problem: in many cultures, actual men are equated with man as such. Some languages even have only one word for both (*homme* in French, for example). Men implicitly stand for humanity, whereas women are considered to be somehow derivative, deficient, inferior human beings.

The practical consequences vary depending on the region of the world, the prevailing ideology, and the era: women may have, for example, fewer rights, less money, minimal experience of public life, and limited access to positions of power. Or—in emancipated societies—if they are considered to be "equals," they are still measured against a male norm.

This primacy of the male is called *patriarchy* (literally: rule by the father) and it exists in many variants. Its core hierarchy structures almost every other form of power, not just the relationship between the genders: the head of the household over his children, maids, and servants; the free man over slaves; "natives" over immigrants; the "better off" over the "lower classes," and so on.

Understanding the causes of patriarchy and how exactly it has come about has been controversial. Some believe it is the result of historical developments that began about 5,000 years ago with the gradual displacement of early indigenous cultures. Some believe patriarchy is the inevitable consequence of the fact that not everyone can get pregnant and give birth, resulting in a gendered division of labor that emerged at the expense of women. Others reject the term "patriarchy" altogether because it gathers too many diverse phenomena under one label.

Indeed, there is such a variety of "patriarchal" societies that the term is insufficient for the purposes of analyzing concrete conditions. But they do all have something in common. Every patriarchal society has feminism—which is to say, they have a number of people, more often women than men, who reject the notion that the masculine is superior to the feminine in their culture and who argue for the liberation of women.

Feminism is not so much a fixed program as an attitude. Feminists see gender difference as an important analytic tool without which social processes and relations cannot be understood. Their activism is guided by the criterion of the liberation of women, and this liberation has a value for them per se: an aim that needs no further justification.

Apart from this, different feminists have very different and sometimes even opposing points of view. These viewpoints are always shaped by specific issues and the specific problems of the time—and, of course, by the subjective ideas and views of the thinker or activist concerned.

To understand feminist ideas, then, we must always look at them in their proper context and not boil them down to one simple definition. Individuals will inevitably have to form their own judgments and take their own positions. There can be no one "feminism." New propositions, discoveries, and findings are emerging all the time.

Some of these ideas and developments are laid out in this book. The focus here is European, Western feminism, because that's the tradition in which the authors are knowledgeable and, thus, the discourse to which this book belongs. Feminism has long existed everywhere else in the world, but that feminism may look quite different from the feminism presented here.

A Brief History of
Feminism

ANTIQUITY

The very earliest known texts from ancient Europe—ancient Greece and ancient Rome to be precise—are already the texts of patriarchal societies. Therefore, nearly all of the philosophical and political ideas that have come down to us are men's ideas; only very few texts from this period can be definitely identified as authored by women. The ideas women dreamt up, the concerns they prioritized at the time, the thoughts they had on human coexistence—unfortunately, we have to remain in the dark about all that.

Yes, and that's a good thing too. *A man who teaches a woman how to read or write is ill-advised, for he is providing extra venom to an asp.*

Menander, 342/341 BC, Greek playwright

We do have some fragmentary traces of certain women. For example, we know that a poet called Sappho lived on the isle of Lesbos in the 7th or 6th century BCE. She wrote poems about love and sensuality.

We also know a little about the philosopher Ptolemais, who wrote a book on the "Pythagorean principles of music" around the 3rd century BCE. Plato also mentions the philosopher Diotima, allegedly a teacher of Socrates, but her historical existence has not been verified.

The Hebrew Bible features several important women, such as the prophet Miriam and the political leader Esther. There are also important women in the New Testament such as the Apostles Junia, Thekla, and Mary Magdalene.

Do you really want to make Peter your deputy?

Yes, why not?

Well, you're a man, he's a man... People will end up thinking you don't want women to be priests.

Really, Mary, do you always have to be so negative?

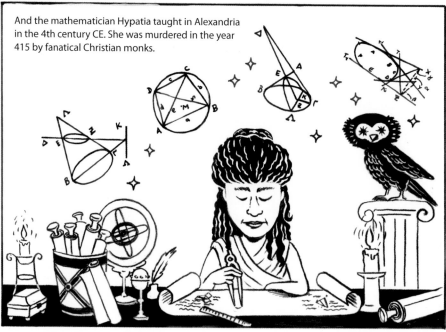

And the mathematician Hypatia taught in Alexandria in the 4th century CE. She was murdered in the year 415 by fanatical Christian monks.

Because we have no substantive texts from this period we can say women authored with 100% certainty, we can only indirectly infer what women's ideas actually were.

For instance, take a look at a moment from the life of the early Christian missionary Paul:

Right, before I forget, this is very important: Women should be SILENT in church congregations.

Whereas in reality . . .

Paul's rebuke would not have been necessary if women had, in fact, always been silent in church.

Throughout antiquity, men penned texts admonishing women to lead a chaste life, to submit to men and especially their husbands, to fulfill their domestic duties, not make any demands, and so on.

The fact that these injunctions were necessary shows that there was, at least, some controversy around the matter, and that women didn't all simply fall in line.

As I keep saying: A woman should be seen and not heard. Somehow it hasn't had much effect.

Sophocles, 5th cent. BCE, Greek poet

There seems to have been a somewhat broader discussion about the role of women in society during the 2nd and 3rd centuries. Some of the texts from the philosophical school of "Gnosticism" elaborate the idea of a quasi-ungendered spirituality and knowledge that women can attain too, if they "become like men."

And how, if you please, was that supposed to work? Perhaps like this?

Ha ha! You can't be as enlightened as us! You don't have a penis.

Dear God, I'm just a weak woman, but please help me become male!

Okay, just this once!

4

FEMINISM IN THE MIDDLE AGES

In the Middle Ages, Christianity gradually became the predominant worldview in Europe.

Look out, here come the Christians!

God chose me to be his representative on Earth!

No he didn't! He chose meee!

They're getting on my nerves! I think I'll hang out with you.

Although the church was a strictly hierarchical and purely male organization, many women refused to subordinate themselves to this hierarchy. They did not reject Christianity wholesale, however. Instead, they claimed a form of direct access to God, independent from the clergy—through visions, for example, and mystical insights. They often justified this by arguing that a church doctrine created by men could never be valid for for them as women.

For example, the German Abbess Hildegard von Bingen (1098–1170) engaged in numerous conflicts with the reigning powers (both secular and ecclesiastical) of her time. She invoked visions, which gave her insight into a higher, cosmological order.

If God is male, then the male is God.

Right on, man!

Mary Daly (1928–2010), originally a Catholic theologian, was one of the most important thinkers in feminist theology in the 20th century. Her 1973 book *Beyond God the Father* influenced many women. Daly herself later turned her back on the church.

Many mystics claimed that it was easier for women to "have direct access to God" (today we would say: "know what action is right") because they had no involvement in the secular power structures.

Some openly challenged the church hierarchy. One such woman was Wilhelmina of Milan, who had a vision in 1280.

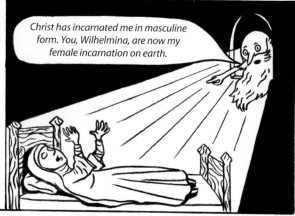

Christ has incarnated me in masculine form. You, Wilhelmina, are now my female incarnation on earth.

Two years later . . .

Mayfreda, I'm going to die soon. Finish what I have started. You must create a church with a female hierarchy.

However, Wilhelmina's followers were denounced to the Inquisition and Mayfreda was burned as a heretic in 1300.

Generally speaking, from the 13th century on, women in Europe demonstrated a stronger need for community life—life beyond marriage and monasteries. Women lived together in pairs or in smaller collectives, working together, or else formed larger organized convents with up to one hundred members. Others traveled through the country, singly or in groups.

Soon "Beguines" came into being. Some of these communities had no fixed rules, while others had very precise contracts for those who wished to join them. Most of the Beguine convents were financed by the work of their members, whether in the craft sector, in nursing care, or in trade.

One of the best-known Beguines was the Frenchwoman Marguerite Porete (ca. 1260–1310), who wrote the first major spiritual work in the vernacular language (instead of Latin). *The Mirror of Simple Souls* describes how "God" can be found only through "love," not through the church, nor through reason or virtue. Everything depends on the individual's ability to love, that is, to do the right thing in a specific, concrete situation. Laws and abstract rules do not contribute to the good in the world—as such, we might even consider Marguerite Porete an early anarchist. *The Mirror* is not a philosophical tract, but outlines a down-to-earth, experimental praxis (quite similar, in fact, to the literature of the women's movement in the 1970s).

Paris, Whitsun, 1310

Despite widespread repression, her book's influence grew. Latin, English, and Italian translations had already appeared in the 14th century.

While it had tolerated them at first, the church stepped up its persecution of the Beguines in the 14th and 15th centuries. Eventually almost all of the women's collectives were crushed or else forced to transform themselves into monasteries operating under strict ecclesiastical control. Nevertheless, some Beguine communes did survive, all the way into the 19th century.

Even within the newly "official" nunneries, distinct women-led traditions survived. The Spanish abbess Teresa of Ávila (1515–1582), for example, drew up her own rules for the monasteries she founded, because she believed that the orders for men, having been designed by men, were not suitable for women. An inquisitorial proceeding was initiated against her order, but eventually the church recognized her doctrines as orthodox, and canonized Teresa in 1622. In 1970 she became (posthumously) the first woman ever to become a Doctor of the Church.

We should not assess feminist ideas using the criteria of currently dominant ideologies. Just as the medieval church burned many progressive-thinking women at the stake while declaring others saints, neoliberal society now adopts some feminist ideas with gusto, while marginalizing others as totally utopian.

During the Reformation in the 16th century, many nunneries were forcibly disbanded. The women who had been living in them were compelled to marry in order to survive, which in turn meant that many areas suffered the near-total collapse of their independent traditions and ways of life.

A new generation of feminist theologians had to rediscover many of these traditions in the 20th century, since the official church historiographies did not mention them.

EARLY MODERN FEMINISM

In the modern period, ideas of the nation-state, rule of law, and science gradually displaced Christian beliefs. Sadly, however, this did not mean that the standing of women all of a sudden improved. Because, you see, men could now supposedly argue the case for women's inferiority "objectively" . . .

Let us leave God's will and Eve's original sin to one side for a moment . . .

. . . the newest scientific findings have revealed that women are less capable beings, after all.

Yes, and we men of the law can only agree.

One of the most important feminists of the early modern period whose life and work we still know of today was the French philosopher and writer Christine de Pizan (1365–1430). In 1405 she published *The Book of the City of Ladies*, in which she deftly attacks, with an exquisite sense of irony, the misogynist thinking of many of her contemporaries, especially the popular notion that women have fewer aptitudes and are less capable than men.

How can so many men write such horrible things about women?

"They who defame women are small spirits. They have encountered so many women ranking far above them in terms of wisdom and gentility, that their reaction is to be sulky and indignant. And because of this grudge, they speak ill of all women."
—Christine de Pizan

In *City of Ladies* Pizan pays tribute to numerous biblical or historical women and paints a picture of a utopian society in which all women are free and enjoy the same rights as men.

The book represents one of the less typical contributions to the so-called Woman Question, a Europe-wide debate over the essence and status of women, which lasted from the 14th right through to the 18th century. The spectrum of opinion ranged from those who outright denied that women are people and saw women as being on a level with animals, all the way to those who defended the dignity of women and championed their freedom.

In general, perspectives on the "Woman Question" became more polarized in this period. On the one hand, hatred of women increased, and this found its ultimate expression in the persecution of witches. On the other hand, subcultures developed in which women could have relatively powerful influence, for example, the "Précieuses," a movement among the nobility.

An important early thinker in this movement was the French philosopher Marie de Gournay (1565–1645).

Biological differences in sex do not account for the spirit of a human being, rather, they serve only for procreation. After all, this female cat on my windowsill cannot be distinguished from a tomcat.

A logical consequence is the right of women to be human, for in principle the human spirit is neither masculine nor feminine.

Her book *The Equality of Men and Women* appeared in 1622. It's a very early example of modern "equal rights" discourse: a truly visionary text for its time.

Indeed, in a strongly hierarchical society that was divided into "estates," the very idea of equality (not just between sexes, but among human beings in general) was seen as completely absurd. Gournay suffered a lot of scorn and derision in the wake of her intervention.

"Most of those who take up the cause of women, opposing the arrogant preference for themselves that is asserted by men, give them full value for money, for they redirect the preference to them. For my part, I fly all extremes, I am content to make them equal to men." —Marie de Gournay

FEMINISM IN THE ENLIGHTENMENT

Wake up! Reason knows no gender!

Only with the Enlightenment in the 18th century did the idea of human equality spread in Europe, especially with the French Revolution of 1789.

Many women took part in the uprisings. For example, the famous Women's March on Versailles on October 5, 1789, in which over 8,000 working and bourgeois women participated, became the stuff of legend.

We are protesting against flour and bread shortages!

The King must finally abdicate!

However, the main cry of the Revolution went like this:

Liberty, equality, fraternity!

But fraternity means brotherhood! So is this equality we all demand not intended for women?

Human = man, yeah?!

It got even worse: the more men began to regard one another as equals, the more formidable the inequality faced by women became.

According to this logic, gender was no longer just one of many characteristics by which groups of people could be differentiated. It was now imbued with a privileged significance. The main argument went like this:

In the course of revolutions, we frequently find a marked pattern. When new social movements arise, women are usually centrally involved. At this stage, women are engaged, they demonstrate, they fight.

But if the revolution is "successful," if the old rulers have been dethroned, and new forms of government have arisen, then men come to dominate again. This mechanism is an important area of feminist inquiry: where does this male preference for institutional power come from?

Why do women put up with this exclusion?

Might the skepticism and aversion felt by many women in relation to formal forms of power and institutions prove quite "useful" in the construction of postrevolutionary societies?

Let me think about it for a minute.

"*I may excite laughter, by dropping an hint, which I mean to pursue some future time, for I really think women ought to have representatives, instead of being arbitrarily governed without having any direct share allowed them in the deliberations of government.*"

—Mary Wollstonecraft

In 1818, Mary Shelley (daughter of Mary Wollstonecraft) wrote the international best-seller *Frankenstein*, a masterpiece on the hubris of modern science that remains relevant to this day.

From the beginning, feminists have protested against the idea that one might posit human equality as an ideal while simultaneously excluding half of humanity. Two of the best known are Mary Wollstonecraft and Olympe de Gouges.

As early as 1790 the English teacher and writer Mary Wollstonecraft (1759–1797) wrote a book on human rights. In 1792 she traveled to Paris to get a sense of the consequences of the Revolution on the ground.

Woman is expressly made to please man.

Jean-Jacques Rousseau (1712–1778), French philosopher

Just you wait 'til my new book comes out, Jean-Jacques!

In Paris she wrote *A Vindication of the Rights of Women*. In so doing she was one of the first to criticize the fact that women were raised and socialized to be dependents. She was elaborating an argument that for many feminists remains pressing to this day: that the actually existing differences between men and women don't have "natural" causes but are produced, in the first instance, by society.

In 1791, the French artist and human rights activist Marie Gouze (1748–1793), better known by her pen name Olympe de Gouges, wrote the *Declaration of the Rights of Woman and the Female Citizen*.

She had been forced into marriage at seventeen and developed her political consciousness at an early age. Even before the French Revolution she campaigned for the abolition of slavery, divorce rights, and other social issues.

Women! Isn't it about time that a revolution should take place among ourselves as well? Are we to remain isolated from one another in eternity?

> *Any society in which the guarantee of rights is not assured or the separation of powers not settled has no constitution. The constitution is null and void*

> *if the majority of individuals composing the nation has not cooperated in its drafting.*

Her best-known "bon mot"—a woman who has the right to ascend to the scaffold must also have the right to ascend a political platform—came all too true for Olympe de Gouges. On account of her political opinions on Robespierre's regime of terror, like so many others, she was executed by guillotine in 1793.

EARLY SOCIALIST FEMINISM

At the beginning of the 19th century it became clearer and clearer that the idea of the "equality of all men" had not only widened the chasm between men and women . . .

. . . but also that between rich and poor.

For political equality did not reflect the real conditions of life. Rather, it only provided the rich with even more of an excuse to focus exclusively on their own interests . . .

The insufficiency of legal equality was the reason why various socialist movements came into being, whose dreams of equality pointed to a greater social and material kind of justice. Some socialists founded communes and projects in which they experimented with new forms of working and living together.

What is remarkable about this historic movement is not only the sheer number of women who were personally active in it, but the fact that almost *all* early socialist theories and projects explicitly addressed the question of the relation between the sexes. The gender question played an especially central role in Saint-Simonism, among the followers of the sociologist Henri de Saint-Simon, who died in 1825.

Buchez, I say to you: the new world will be governed by a papal couple. The female pope will represent emotion and the male pope reason. It's the only way a peaceful society can arise.

That man must liberate woman, and that women must be represented in all public offices, are things that we all agree on.

But there's one thing you're mistaken about, Enfantin: what you call gender-specific characteristics are not in fact "given" by nature, but rather, are attributable to unequal socialization.

While the men were still quarreling . . .

I've had enough of these men who think they can speak for us.

Yes, Saint-Simonism is still colored by male perspectives.

Let's publish our own newspaper and set up women's groups.

Some Saint-Simonist women signaled their revolutionary thinking via daring forms of vestimentary self-expression, for example by wearing noticeably short skirts, which displayed the fact that they were wearing trousers underneath.

Among the important Saint-Simonist women were Claire Démar (1799–1833) and Jeanne Deroin (1805–1894).

> *Precisely because woman is equal to man but not identical to him, she should participate in the effort for social reforms, and in so doing she will embody the necessary elements that man lacks, such that the endeavor can be complete.*

Jeanne Deroin

They developed models for gender-conscious organizational structures and founded autonomous women's groups. In general, the Saint-Simonists insisted that every public office and function be occupied in each case by one man and one woman. In 1850, Deroin went to jail for six months on charges of political conspiracy.

> *State your first and last name!*

> *Before I answer, I must protest against the law by which you propose to judge me. It has been been made by men and I do not recognize its authority.*

Their main argument for equal rights was that women can never be truly represented by men and must have their own voice, on the grounds that men and women are different and do not have the same preferences and interests. In this, they were reacting to the lack of contemporary theorizing on formal equality.

The most important theorist of early socialism was Flora Tristan (1803–1844). In 1825 she fled her violent husband.

He pursued her with all available legal means and later even made an attempt on her life.

I may have no legal option to get a divorce, but there's no way in hell I'm staying here.

Her revolutionary ideas must be stopped. I'll kill her before she destroys the foundations of our society!

Tristan fought back, rallying support and causing a great stir in France.

On a trip to Peru, where her family had property, Tristan rebelled against slavery and class exploitation.

STOP!!

He deserves it. He stole from me and lied about it.

As though enslaving humans were not the greatest theft imaginable! Can you expect virtue from someone who isn't allowed to have free will of their own?

The slave doesn't owe his or her master anything, and on the contrary, has the right to move against him in any way.

In 1840, she traveled to London and researched the living conditions of workers under capitalism. She reflected on both of these experiences in her books.

"Workers, try hard to understand this: the law that subjugates women and deprives them of education oppresses you, you, proletarian men."—Flora Tristan

In 1843—five years before Marx and Engels published *The Communist Manifesto*—Tristan's main oeuvre *The Workers' Union* was published, in which she not only championed the idea of a union of male and female workers that would transcend guilds and professional branches, but also drew an analytic link between the oppression of women and the oppression of the proletariat. She promoted her ideas throughout France via lecture tours, up until her early death from typhoid in 1844.

BEGINNINGS OF AN ORGANIZED WOMEN'S MOVEMENT

Up until the middle of the 19th century, individual feminist actors and women's groups had certainly mobilized around specific issues, or unionized in certain trades. But there hadn't been anything like an organized women's movement.

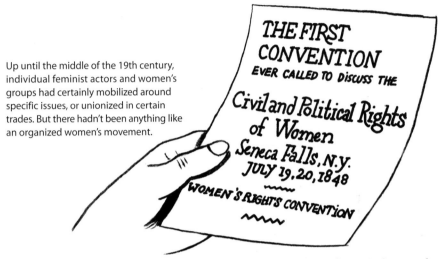

THE FIRST CONVENTION EVER CALLED TO DISCUSS THE Civil and Political Rights of Women Seneca Falls, N.Y. JULY 19, 20, 1848 WOMEN'S RIGHTS CONVENTION

Accordingly it caused quite a stir when US feminists organized a two-day conference in the state of New York.

The two initiators . . .

In almost all congresses and political debates women are not allowed to participate as delegates, and sometimes may not even enter the room! In future this has to stop, Elizabeth!

Exactly, my dear! Our goal will be to get women more social and political influence.

Lucrezia Mott (1793–1880), women's rights activist and Quaker.

Elizabeth Cady Stanton (1815–1902), civil and women's rights activist.

Approximately 300 people interested parties attended the Seneca Falls Convention and supported its demands, including some men—for example, the black civil rights activist Frederick Douglass (1818–1895).

I'm for women's right to vote!

Women as politicians in parliament? Isn't that a bit too radical?

Women have to pay taxes, don't they? Then why shouldn't they participate fully in politics?

At the end of the convention, a "Declaration of Rights and Sentiments" was adopted, revoking all claims to power over women, in explicit reference to the American Declaration of Independence.

Thomas Jefferson wrote in his Declaration of Independence that all men are created equal. And we are hereby declaring that all men and women are also created equal by Nature and are therefore endowed with the same rights!

"We insist that women have immediate admission to all the rights and privileges which belong to them as citizens of these United States. In entering upon the great work before us, we anticipate no small amount of misconception, misrepresentation, and ridicule; but we shall use every instrumentality within our power to effect our object."—Elizabeth Cady Stanton

In Europe, too, feminists set up numerous women's associations in the second half of the 19th century, and several national and international assemblies took place. At the same time, among male intellectuals, an increasingly "antifeminist" mood began to spread. This backlash was antifeminist in the original sense of the word: namely, "against women."

Political activists, writers, and intellectuals such as Jules Michelet, Pierre-Joseph Proudhon, Auguste Comte, and many many others, rejected women's demands for political and social codetermination.

This concentrated wave of antiwoman sentiment provoked, in turn, a wave of feminist literature. Feminists took apart the crude propositions of the antifeminists, both seriously and, on occasion, lightheartedly, through the use of sarcasm. Particularly popular in France was an essay by Juliette Adam (1836–1936) published in 1858: "Anti-Proudhonist Ideas about Love, Woman and Marriage"; and later, in Germany, a book titled *The Antifeminists* (1902) by Hedwig Dohm (1831–1919).

"Our enemies come at us from above as from below. By which I mean: they can justify their opposition by reference to either the spiritual or bodily inferiority of Woman, or else, disguise it by invoking the lofty mission of Woman as the mother-priestess of home and hearth, her tender gentleness and all the rest of it. The majority, however, deploy both tactics simultaneously: belt and braces, as it were. For the most part—leaving aside, of course, all ethical and aesthetic feelings of repugnance—their argumentation consists of mere assertion." —Hedwig Dohm

At the US women's conference in 1851, the itinerant preacher and former slave Sojourner Truth (1798–1883) gave one of the most impressive speeches of the time, which not only debunked the idea of "positive discrimination" favoring women as a "weaker" sex in need of protection, but simultaneously denounced the racism inherent in those bourgeois clichés about gender in the first place.

Three topical concerns preoccupied the emerging women's unions and women's groups of that era: the demand for better access to paid work; the critique of traditional households and the injustice of forced marriage (a critique often bound up with ideas of "free love"); and the demand for universal suffrage.

WOMEN'S WAGE LABOR

The most important issue for women's movements in the 19th century was women's entry into the wage labor market. In fact, at the outset of industrialization—which began in the textiles sector—the majority of workers had been women.

> What are you staring at? After all, I can't help it if our pay is worse than yours!

> Yes, they should just let us join their union, instead of seeing us as the competition. We obviously want to be paid better too!

But the more factory work grew in general importance, the more the male workers' associations and labor unions demanded a ban or at least restrictions on female factory work. The First International (1864–1872) itself—the first umbrella organization representing the European laboring class—passed motions along these lines at its first congresses, and only arrived at a more moderate position later on.

Meanwhile, among bourgeois women, the situation looked different . . .

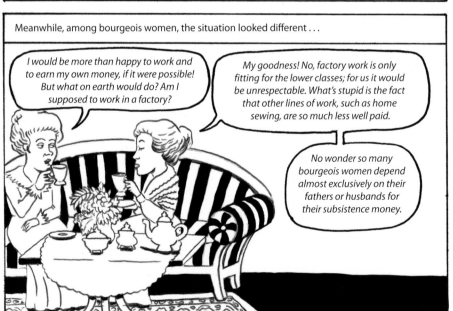

> I would be more than happy to work and to earn my own money, if it were possible! But what on earth would do? Am I supposed to work in a factory?

> My goodness! No, factory work is only fitting for the lower classes; for us it would be unrespectable. What's stupid is the fact that other lines of work, such as home sewing, are so much less well paid.

> No wonder so many bourgeois women depend almost exclusively on their fathers or husbands for their subsistence money.

For this reason, the question of access to adequately paid and respectable opportunities for wage labor occupied a central position in almost all feminist activities during these years. Feminists organized practical initiatives for self-help, discussed the issue in economic terms, and set up lobbies to push for the appropriate political measures.

In doing so, they mostly rejected all so-called "women's protection laws" that legally prohibited women from working certain jobs on account of their (supposedly fragile) physical constitutions or their capacity to give birth. Here's one example out of many:

The initiative encountered massive opposition from male printers and trade unions, especially since the venture played hardball when it came to setting prices to attract clients.

In Germany, one journalist and feminist who advocated passionately for women's right to wage labor was Louise Otto-Peters (1819–1895). She launched the *Women's Newspaper* in 1849 (under the famous motto "I am recruiting female citizens for the realm of freedom!"), but went on to found workers' and servants' unions too, and published her book *Women's Right to Earn a Living* in 1866.

Together with others, Otto-Peters organized the first German women's conference in Leipzig in 1865. She directed the General German Women's Union for three decades after that—which offered, for instance, advanced training courses for women.

My objective is, on the one hand, to support women workers in realizing their right to paid work, and, at the same time, to win them over as comrades in the struggle for women's political rights.

"Gentlemen! In the name of morality, in the name of the fatherland, in the name of humanity I appeal to you: when it comes to the organization of labor, do not forget women!"—Louise Otto-Peters

Finally, some important theorists of women's paid labor were Harriet Taylor Mill (1807–1858) her daughter Helen Taylor (1831–1907).

Together with the theorist of liberal political economy John Stuart Mill, which is to say, their husband and stepfather (respectively), they authored numerous texts on economics, as well as on suffrage rights and divorce rights. Their approach to capitalism was utilitarian and oriented toward the "greatest good of the greatest number."

For indeed, women's free participation in labor markets will increase the wealth of any nation!

The close link between the liberal conception of the economy and the demand for unrestricted equality for women is present in all of the Mills's works, but is most explicitly formulated in 1869 in the collectively authored book *The Subjection of Women* (which, however, appeared solely under John Stuart's name).

Are you sure we should do this without your names?

Yes. If we publish under your name, our ideas will gain more recognition and provoke more attention.

"The legal subordination of one sex to the other is wrong in itself, and now one of the chief hindrances to human improvement." —John Stuart Mill, Harriet Taylor Mill, and Helen Taylor

FREE LOVE / THE CRITIQUE OF MARRIAGE

Another crucial theme in the 19th century was the plight of wives. In most European countries, marriage meant a mass transfer of entitlements from bride to groom, and married women lost practically all their rights.

Will you honor and obey this man, in sickness and in health, until death do you part?

Yes, she will!

And cede unto him your choice of living place, control over your your assets, and possibly also your income, in the event that he gives your permission to work? If so, answer now: "I will."

HUHH??

"Husband and wife are one and that is he." (From England's law ordinance on marriage.)

At the time, when it came to marriage, what kind of choice did a bourgeois Woman really have?

Marriage for me was the only possible source of food. Now, without my husband's written permission, I cannot sign any contracts, do any kind of business, appear as a witness in court, nor even travel abroad. And of course he has full, unilateral decision-making power over everything to do with our children.

It was particularly extreme in France, where the Code Civil even expressly prohibited husbands from granting general power of attorney to their wives. Sharing power of attorney had been a key strategy for enlightened couples, not least for practical reasons. Getting a divorce was basically impossible in France, and subject to strict conditions in other countries as well—all of which worked to the disadvantage of the woman. The situation was slightly different in Germany. Until 1874, German weddings were almost exclusively administered by the churches (who often denied people the right to marry).

These marriage laws affected women of different social classes in different ways.

We proletarian women often live with men, outside of marriage, and it is not uncommon for us to then choose other men, or women, to be our life partners.

In our households there simply isn't anything worth inheriting or distributing, so what would be the point of a big song and dance around marriage?

Sex before marriage, for example, just isn't a big deal as far as we're concerned. It's pregnancy you have to worry about. After all, pregnancy has financial implications.

Besides, it was much rarer for people from the proletarian class to hash out their differences before the courts, and deviations from the classical institution of marriage were simply not regarded as particularly scandalous.

In contrast, the bourgeoisie placed enormous emphasis on womanly "respectability." When bourgeois women left their husbands, they faced not only poverty but the loss of their children and the severance of all their social connections. For this reason, the reform of marriage law was really only a concern for bourgeois feminists—the more so because it also encompassed their right to inherit.

If I get a divorce, I will lose the assets I inherited from my father. I am not legally competent to own them in the eyes of the law.

While their attempts at reform remained unsuccessful in France throughout the 19th century, in England the issue was vigorously debated and campaigners secured a couple of ameliorations in 1857 and 1870.

Many feminists did not care particularly about the legal ins and outs of marriage, but wanted to mount a critique of the sexual morality underlying the laws. Some, like the French writer George Sand (1804–1876), lived promiscuous lifestyles and did not hide this from the public. Others, such as the US feminist and socialist Victoria Woodhull (1838–1927), went on the offensive and demanded women's right to sexual autonomy.

"Yes, I am a Free Lover. I have an inalienable, constitutional and natural right to love whom I may, to love as long or as short a period as I can; to change that love every day if I please, and with that right neither you nor any law you can frame have any right to interfere."
—Victoria Woodhull

The Russian "Nihilists," many of whose members used to travel to Western Europe at the time to study, elicited a particularly strong public reaction. They organized a lot of fake weddings between themselves and like-minded men, because single women were not permitted to leave Russia. They advocated dissolving all gendered norms, refused to wear typically feminine clothing, and cultivated a "masculine" lifestyle and habitus.

Within feminism itself, such practices were not met with undivided support. Only a minority of advocates for women's rights wanted to abolish the traditional family entirely. With regard to "free love," the various women's associations and unions did not pull together by any means; they even fought each other over it.

In Germany, for example, by the end of the 19th century three distinct streams had emerged:

The "Radicals" around Minna Cauer (1841–1922), Lida Gustava Heymann (1868–1943), Anita Augspurg (1857–1943), and Helene Stöcker (1869–1943) ...

We demand a new sexual moral order, and a social status for women that is entirely unrelated to marriage.

... the "Moderates" around Helene Lange (1848–1930) and Gertrud Bäumer (1873–1954) ...

We are certainly also for the abolition of forced marriages and unjust laws. Nevertheless, we hold woman's social role as a mother to be important. The aims of feminist emancipation must have their limits.

... and, finally, the "Conservatives," who wanted to valorize the "housewife's vocation" and had no fundamental criticisms of the marital system.

WOMEN'S RIGHT TO VOTE AND PARTY POLITICS

The feminist positions around voting rights were just as polarized. This campaign, too, lay closest to bourgeois women's hearts. In the 19th century, in many countries, the right to vote was still tied to property or land assets, so that most proletarian men were equally as shut out from voting as were women of all classes.

Moreover, many socialist currents, for instance anarchism, aimed at more radical forms of social revolution and generally opposed circumscribing workers' struggles within party apparatuses and the horizons of parliamentary politics.

In the United States, this question even led to a split in the women's movement. There, after the end of the Civil War between the Northern and Southern states in 1869, suffrage rights were introduced for black men—but not for women.

Your privileges? Soon enough you will try to offer us those dull trinkets, in an attempt to restore their former luster by sharing them with us. Keep them, we don't want them.

Louise Michel, French anarchist (1830–1905)

Which is not to say that we will tolerate that happening in the South! We would rather support votes for women!

Many feminists still welcomed this change, because they considered it an important step for the black population. On the other hand, radical women's rights advocates like Susan B. Anthony (1820–1906) or Elizabeth Cady Stanton (1815–1902) were indignant, because they now foresaw women's suffrage being kicked even further down the road as a result. Nor did they shy away from the crudest forms of racism in making their complaint, for instance when they ridiculed the fact that "Sambo" was now allowed to vote, while educated ladies could not. Elizabeth Cady Stanton opined . . .

Toward the end of the 19th century, feminists supported the fight for women's suffrage in ever greater numbers, and increasingly found that they had allies among men. Those most often making the headlines were the English suffragettes, whose imaginative direct action and downright militancy forced the issue into the mainstream. The time had well and truly come: in almost all nation-states, women were admitted into the electorate, for example in 1902 in Australia, 1906 in Finland, 1913 in Norway, 1915 in Denmark, 1918 in Poland, Germany, and Austria, 1920 in the United States, 1928 in the UK, 1930 in Turkey, 1945 in France and Italy, and 1971 in Switzerland.

One of the lasting consequences of debates around women's suffrage was a stronger focus on women's relationship to political party structures.

Now that you're a voter, and you can run for political office, who will enjoy your loyalty? Your party, to whom you feel you belong politically...?

...or perhaps we should put our hopes in a cross-party women's federation.

The beginning of the 20th century saw the proliferation of women's associations specifically affiliated with particular political parties or religious denominations. For example, one of the greatest contributors to socialist feminist organizing in Germany at the time was Clara Zetkin (1857–1933) and her newspaper *Equality*.

The bourgeois women's movement is not the representative or champion of the interests of all women who long for liberation. It is and remains a bourgeois class movement.

These women advocated within their organizations for the rights and interests of women, while simultaneously attempting to win other women over to their worldview. Even if they did sometimes forge alliances with one another's organizations, they refused—again and again—to see one another as a vehicle of women's true interests.

Others, like the Russian-American activist Emma Goldman (1869–1940) had no time at all for institutional organizing, but she was, after all, an anarchist in the first instance and a feminist only second. Or was it the other way around?

You've seen what the women's movement for voting rights looks like. A bourgeois movement that is, in large part, conservative, puritanical, and even racist. You're asking me not to be suspicious of such a movement?

And if voting changed anything, it would be banned!

I want to see women as free human beings, people who are free in equal measure from the state, the church, society, husbands, family, etc.

Naturally some women are hoping to free themselves from all of that with the help of the right to vote. But who really profits from all this, more than anyone? The majority of women are hoping that the vote helps them become better Christians, housewives, and bourgeois citizens.

In any case, the tension between political orientation, on the one hand, and the desire for solidarity among women across or beyond ideological lines, on the other, has been a constant (and thorny) issue in feminism ever since.

THE "OTHER" SEX?

A further problem that cropped up in tandem with the introduction of women's suffrage was the realization that formal rights did not necessarily ameliorate the social situation for women. The French philosopher Simone de Beauvoir (1908–1986) wrote the major groundbreaking book on this theme in 1949.

Even nowadays it's still alleged that there is some kind of natural essence of woman.

I have never felt myself to be inferior. So far I have always lived my life unconventionally and independently. Nevertheless, "being a woman" relegates every woman to secondary status.

In *The Second Sex*, she examines Western European cultural and philosophical history in order to show that gender roles are hammered out, not only on the level of legislation, but in literature, morality, and everyday custom.

"For a long time I have hesitated to write a book on woman. The subject is irritating, especially to women; and it is not new. After all, is there a problem? And if so, what is it? Are there women, really?"—Simone de Beauvoir

"*One is not born but rather becomes a woman*" is probably Beauvoir's most famous line. According to this perspective, the concept of sex is shaped by culture, and does not simply inhere in "*the nature of things.*"

Nor did she conceal the reality that women's passive and subordinate role is not solely assigned to them by men; in fact, women play a major part in maintaining it.

Half victim, half accomplice, just like everybody else.

Politically, she demanded that women be liberated from their social role as mothers, above all; she called on women to put more energy into their professional or political careers and to take steps to ensure that gender differences would disappear from society by and by.

But Simone de Beauvoir became a major icon of feminism only around twenty years later, when she was rediscovered by a newly reinvigorated women's movement.

Now, as then, a majority of feminists share de Beauvoir's cultural analysis. But not everybody agrees with the conclusions she drew. One of those to take issue with them was the French psychoanalyst Luce Irigaray (1930–).

De Beauvoir holds up the male mode of living as though it were the norm, and simply calls on women to adapt themselves to it.

In her 1974 book *Speculum of the Other Woman*, Irigaray demonstrates that masculinity does not merely structure culture: rather, it undergirds the very "symbolic order" and language itself.

Women must now find a language of their own and build a free feminine subjectivity. Only then will it be possible for men and women to enter into a relationship with one another.

In order for the fact of sexual difference to be realized, there will have to be a revolution in thought and ethics. Everything must be signified anew, but we must begin with the Subject, who has hitherto always been specified as masculine, even if we have pretended that it was neutral and universal.

These two positions gave rise to a broad and ever-evolving feminist debate about the relation between "equality" and "difference"—a debate that is still going on today.

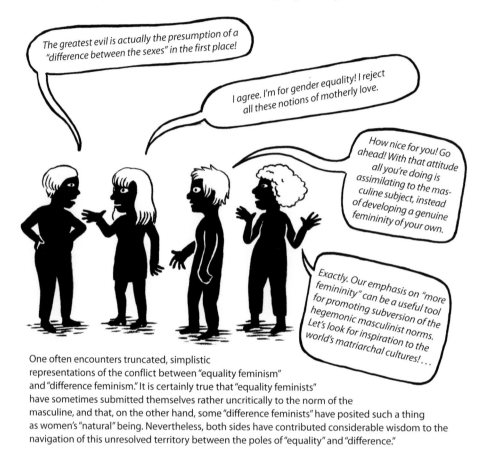

One often encounters truncated, simplistic representations of the conflict between "equality feminism" and "difference feminism." It is certainly true that "equality feminists" have sometimes submitted themselves rather uncritically to the norm of the masculine, and that, on the other hand, some "difference feminists" have posited such a thing as women's "natural" being. Nevertheless, both sides have contributed considerable wisdom to the navigation of this unresolved territory between the poles of "equality" and "difference."

AUTONOMOUS WOMEN'S MOVEMENTS

In tandem with the student movements of the end of the 1960s in the United States and Europe, an autonomous women's movement reconstituted itself as well. "Autonomous" here refers to the fact that the feminists no longer felt committed to their organizations, parties, or religious denominations, but turned instead toward a form of consciousness based on self-organizing simply as women. This turn was prompted by their frustrations about even the most "revolutionary" mixed movements being dominated by men.

Here's a working group in the "Springer campaign" of 1967 (which targeted the right-wing German media giant) . . .

We must expose the manipulation of the working classes by the mass media!

You've forgotten something crucial!

We need an analysis of the way the media treat women!

TODAY'S TIP FOR WOMEN
Here's how you can make a cozy home for your husband on next to no money

Go to the kitchen! Marianne is doing something along those lines there.

The SDS (Socialist German Students' Union) analyses of class society aren't wrong, they're just a bit limited.

Yeah, I think so too. The comrades just haven't yet grasped that the private sphere and its inherently gendered division of labor are political.

In Germany, the filmmaker Helke Sander (1937–) helped found the Action Committee for the Liberation of Women.

In Frankfurt in September 1968, at a plenary meeting of the radical leftist group SDS, this conflict infamously broke out in the form of a "tomato attack." After Sander had given a speech putting forward the demands of the Action Committee, the men summarily tried to switch over to other topics without any further discussion. So, Sigrid Rüger, who was in the audience, threw a tomato that happened to be in her shopping bag at the comrades on the speaker's platform, forcing even the most reluctant to have the discussion.

"After we'd been active for about half a year, most comrades still reacted to what we were doing with scorn. Today, they resent the fact that we withdrew from their movements. They still want to tell us that our social theorizing is completely wrongheaded to begin with. They bang on about how they are oppressed too, which of course isn't news to us. We just aren't willing to put up with their oppression's priority anymore. Their oppression is itself the means by which they oppress us— and we have suffered it without a murmur."

—Helke Sander

In the 1970s, the praxis of "separatism" led to a groundswell of women's groups, women's bookstores, and women's cafés, not only in metropolitan areas, but also in many small towns. It was US feminists who invented "consciousness-raising," whereby women would speak among themselves, sharing their experiences with each other and reflecting on them politically. Women's groups in many other countries also adopted this practice.

Lesbian women played a vital role in the "second wave" of feminism. Many of the women who pioneered the new projects were lesbians, perhaps because, since they were already conducting their private relationships in a "woman-identified" way, their everyday lives could easily be combined with feminist-separatist praxis. Of course, women had lived together as couples long before that (for example, Lida Gustava Heymann and Anita Augspurg), but during the first wave no one had turned their lesbianism into a subject for political discussion.

The theorization of lesbianism was hugely advanced by the French writer Monique Wittig (1935–2005). From her point of view, lesbians were not women at all: *"it would be incorrect to say that lesbians associate, make love, live with women, for 'woman' has meaning only in heterosexual systems of thought and heterosexual economic systems. Lesbians are not women."*

In the course of their feminist engagements, lesbians also intensified their criticisms of men's dominance within the gay movement.

For us, it's not about getting acceptance for "same-sex love."

We want sexed concepts to be challenged in general!

Many of us think of our lesbianism not so much as a sexual identity, but as a political statement.

OK. Are you ready now?

Uh-huh. I think so.

Women, who had previously lived their love for other women in secret, now made their relationships public.

Others who had previously lived with men and also poured their energies into motherhood now decided—as a result of their engagement with the feminist movement—to share their intimate lives with women as well. Such people were known as "movement lesbians." As one popular slogan put it:

At the beginning of the 1980s, the US poet and cultural theorist Adrienne Rich (1929–2012) developed the concept of the "lesbian continuum." She directed her analysis at "compulsory heterosexuality" and posited that female homosexuality is taboo—in a patriarchal culture—because it reveals the belief that women can only find true fulfillment in a relationship with a man to be a lie. As such, according to Rich, lesbianism really concerns all women.

"I mean the term lesbian continuum to include a range—through each woman's life and throughout history—of woman-identified experience; not simply the fact that a woman has had or consciously desired genital sexual experience with another woman."
—Adrienne Rich

Soon thereafter, feminist magazines proliferated, the most well-known ones in Germany being *Courage* (1976–1984) and *Emma* (founded 1977), which is still publishing today.

> *This intense period of awakening for feminists in the 1970s is often called "the second wave" (after the first wave, the fight for women's voting rights).*

In terms of political content, three main battlegrounds became particularly important during this time. All are mutually interrelated: claiming bodily self-determination as a fundamental right; revolutionizing parenting, housework, and domestic labor; and blowing the lid off the scandal of epidemic sexual violence in society.

THE FIGHT FOR AUTONOMOUS PREGNANCY

Shit! What are you going to do now? None of these doctors will help you. Especially since you're not married.

Well I won't go to that other quack. I've heard of women who bled to death on that kitchen table.

Have you heard of the knitting needle method?

Let me stop you right there. I can well imagine what it is. I only know about the "parsley" method.

I got a telephone number from Sarah. When I call, I have to say that I have the same medical condition she had. It'll cost around 500 marks. I have no idea how I'm going to find the money.

This absolutely has to stay between us! If news of my abortion gets out, many people will despise me, and besides, I could go to prison for up to five years.

At this time, one of the most important topics for the feminist movement was physical self-determination, as expressed in the slogan "My Body, My Choice."

Regardless of any laws or prevailing religious dogmas, women WILL have abortions. So the question is not whether there should be abortion in society, but HOW abortion should be.

DOWN WITH CLAUSE 218

MY BODY MY CHOICE!

In April 1971, nearly 350 French women—including celebrities such as Catherine Deneuve and Jeanne Moreau—publicly disclosed the fact that they had had abortions in the pages of *Le Nouvel Observateur*. In Germany, Alice Schwarzer (1942–) initiated an identical intervention in *Stern* magazine in June 1971, in which Senta Berger and Romy Schneider, among others, struck a blow against the nationwide ban on abortion.

Not all of the women who started speaking up about abortion, unashamed, had had abortions themselves. The campaign was really much more a question of demonstrating that the power to make choices about pregnancy concerns all women.

In the United States, feminists supported a class action against the abortion ban in the state of Texas. The Supreme Court had ruled in the case of *Roe v. Wade* in 1973 that any law prohibiting women from having an abortion is unconstitutional as long as the fetus is unable to live on its own.

In East Germany in 1972, the People's Parliament legalized abortion during the first three months of pregnancy. Then, in West Germany, the Parliament resolved in 1974 to follow suit and implement this type of first-trimester legalization. However, that law was buried soon after by the German Constitutional Court.

In some countries today, a "de facto" first-trimester limit on abortion persists. This means that abortion, while officially illegal, is not subject to prosecution under penal law as long as pregnant women conform to certain limits and are willing, for example, to accept counseling.

Abortion after twelve weeks is only legitimate and legal when strictly medical, eugenic, or criminological criteria determine the pregnancy to be "unacceptable for the woman."

That makes it sound like getting an abortion in that time frame is simple and straightforward for everybody. In reality, you have to pay for the procedure yourself, except in so-called "special cases."

I recently heard about a young woman in the United States who tried to crowd-fund her abortion online.

I'm not surprised. I'm denied medical care entirely just because my legal status in this country is irregular. Pregnancy, birth, and—for that matter—abortion would all be very difficult for me.

Some feminists considered the focus on pregnancy a narrowing of contemporary debates. They felt other topics warranted more attention within the feminist struggle. Some of them specifically resented that the demands connected with pregnancy didn't go far enough. The US activist Shulamith Firestone (1945–2012) had already argued for the total abolition of the biological family in her 1970 book *The Dialectic of Sex*, which soon became a best-seller.

In Firestone's vision, people would live in communities in which no special attachment exists between a given mother and child. One of her utopian demands was the transcendence of biological pregnancy by means of reproductive technology. In this way, a society would emerge in which gender differences would no longer play any role.

"Feminists have to question, not just all of Western culture, but the organization of culture itself, and further, even the very organization of nature."
—Shulamith Firestone

Aside from pursuing political demands, women in the 1970s also elaborated systems of practical support. They organized trips to places like the Netherlands, where abortion was legal. They educated themselves and each other about methods of contraception, founded women's health centers, and explored their own bodies—for example, by examining their own vaginas.

DOMESTIC VIOLENCE

A feminist group in the 1970s . . .

I'd never have thought that so many members of our group were experiencing violence in their marriage or domestic partnership.

The second big task in the so-called second wave of feminist activism was to expose domestic violence against women and children.

People are only now beginning to realize that homes are actively dangerous places for many women, and in no sense sanctuaries, as we commonly imagined.

MY HOME IS MY CASTLE

Instances or rape and battery that take place within a marriage are widely understood to be private matters, not criminal acts.

My best bet is to stay silent. If I don't he'll get angry!

And many of the women victimized thought their case was the exception.

She probably provoked him!

You know what marriage is like. Now and then there's fireworks—it's only natural.

The testimonies shared in women's centers and consciousness-raising groups planted the seeds of widespread sensitization to the fact that violence within families isn't limited to individual incidents, but represents a structural problem.

Accordingly, in almost every city in that period, feminists set up independent women's crisis services and shelters, where victims of domestic violence could take refuge without having to file bureaucratic appeals.

On a political level, activists put their energy into criminalizing rape within marriage.

A legal amendment of this nature would only result in it being widely abused by wives. And abortion rates would soar.

It took twenty-five years for the law to be passed.

In 1997, German criminal law was finally amended, making rape within marriage a crime. In the intervening time, many of the autonomous women's refuges and advice centers feminists had set up in the 1970s for victims of violence passed into municipal hands or started receiving public funding.

HOUSEWORK, CARE, MOTHERHOOD

The third central theme of second-wave feminism was the critique of the gendered division of labor. Broadly speaking, within homes, men were in charge of earning money, and women were in charge of (unpaid) housework and the (unpaid) work of raising children.

The Action Committee for the Liberation of Women had called for the abolition of the bourgeois compartmentalization of private life and social life. Its founder Helke Sander was also the cofounder of the "Kinderladen" (playschool) movement, in which mothers and preschool educators conceived of alternative institutions for collectivizing childcare and launched initiatives along those lines. The point of all this was not simply to render the organization of care labor and housework independent of the state. The movement was experimenting with new concepts in liberatory pedagogy—rooted in antiauthoritarian principles—which took the children seriously as subjects.

There was considerable disagreement about the way housework and child care should ideally be structured and economically organized. Some demanded "Wages for Housework," not simply to guarantee housewives an income of their own, but to expose housework's centrality to the national economy. (These feminists' contention, that the ensemble of unpaid cooking, cleaning, washing, and parenting that took place within households constituted real "work" was a radical new idea at the time.) Others demanded that housework and paid work be distributed equally between the sexes; or that housework be thoroughgoingly centralized and professionalized. Over the course of these debates, the putative "naturalness" of motherhood as women's vocation in life and the idea of their innate capacity for care were fatally undermined.

In 1987, a group of women affiliated with the Green Party in Germany published a "Mother's Manifesto," in which they advocated basic economic security for unpaid mothers and the social valorization of housework. Their critics accused them of reinforcing gender stereotypes.

Women! Abandon the ghetto of childlessness and break free of the aquarium of "career womanhood"!

Motherhood isn't just a burden, it's also joy and fulfillment!

In order to make women work for nothing, one cannot very well extol the beauty and glamor of washing dishes and doing the laundry by way of enticement. So, instead, you tell them about the joy motherhood.

Simone de Beauvoir (1908–1986)

In actual fact, society developed in the direction of "gender mainstreaming," the province of paid labor, while housework and care continues to be regarded to this day as a private matter. This priority of paid over unpaid work was entrenched via corresponding changes in the law—for example, substantial reductions in the right to alimony, and the neoliberal reform of children's benefits.

Women's increasing involvement in paid work in the 1990s and 2000s certainly delivered more economic independence and security for some women. But the problem remains that the parameters within which housekeeping and child care take place are highly precarious; in fact, this precarity has only grown worse. While women today work exponentially more paid hours than they did in the 1960s and '70s, men hardly spend more time now than they used to on housekeeping and child care.

So, the question is: who shall do the job formerly known as "housewife," when there are no more housewives? This is a question we still haven't answered. The current situation generates huge amounts of stress because of the "double burden" or "double shift" for mothers who have careers. Other consequences include the outsourcing of all kinds of domestic services to migrant women, who toil under precarious and often legally ambiguous conditions in private households; and—on the other hand—the delegation of care to public institutions, where the high costs incurred often translate into low wages and terrible contracts for the people working in that sector, not to mention poor-quality service.

In all this time, feminist initiatives have continued to grapple with the issue of care. In March 2014, a high-profile political event in Berlin titled "Care Revolution" brought together all the strands of this discussion. A network emerged, which continues to make every effort to put care at the heart of political conversations.

WOMANISM AND INTERSECTIONALITY
AGAINST THE DOMINANCE OF WHITE, BOURGEOIS WOMEN

* A 1932 law in the United States provided a mandate for forced sterilization. In practice, the policy became a vector for the racist population politics espoused by the government. Those affected were overwhelmingly indigenous, Chicana, Puerto Rican, and African-American women.

As early as the 1960s, more and more women raised their voices in criticism of the dominance of a white, bourgeois perspective on women's rights, for example the poet Audre Lorde (1934–1992) . . .

"If white American feminist theory need not deal with the differences between us, and the resulting difference in our oppressions, then how do you deal with the fact that the women who clean your houses and tend your children while you attend conferences on feminist theory are, for the most part, poor women and women of color?"

. . . or the philosopher Angela Davis (1944–), whose book *Women, Race, and Class* was published in 1981.

"As a black woman, my politics and political affiliation are bound up with and flow from participation in my people's struggle for liberation, and with the fight of oppressed people all over the world."

Racist feminists! I can't believe it!

I'm shocked!

To underline these differences, black activist women coined the term "womanism." The linked nature of different relations of discrimination was also dealt with at the time under the term "triple oppression" (which meant the threefold oppression on the basis of sex, skin color, and class affiliation).

At the end of the 1980s, the legal theorist Kimberlé Crenshaw (1959–) coined the term "intersectionality," that is, crossroads. It speaks to the fact that different forms of discrimination can't just be added up: a person is discriminated against as a woman, a person of color, and a lesbian— a lesbian woman of color—all at once. The different axes of oppression are so interlinked that the specific character of each individual aspect transforms the others as well. For example, a black woman is treated differently as a woman than a white woman is.

Kimberlé Crenshaw directed her criticisms at the simplistic understanding of disadvantage embedded in antidiscrimination law. For example: the case of *DeGraffenreid v. General Motors.*

In its mass dismissal, the General Motors company has almost exclusively sacked black women. We're dealing with discriminatory corporate policy.

Your Honor, there is no discrimination here. Why, in the same department, we still employ women, and black men.

Case dismissed.

The terminology proliferates . . .

Originally, there were the three categories of race, class, and gender.

We cannot simply lift the American category of race and apply it to the European context.

Furthermore, it soon became clear that besides these three, numerous other kinds of systemic injustice demanded analysis, for example, discrimination on the basis of sexual orientation, bodily norms, age, and so on.

Today, in feminism, to take an intersectional approach is basically indispensable. At the same time, things are not going so smoothly. .

GENDER MAINSTREAMING AND THE PROMOTION OF WOMEN

In the 1980s, women in many countries began to advocate for the de facto equality for women within political institutions, and to launch corresponding legal initiatives.

The United Nations' Fourth World Conference on Women in Beijing in 1995 went down in history as a red-letter day. Official delegates from 189 countries took part. The result of the discussions was a platform through which the nation-states committed themselves to promoting equality between women and men in the political, economic, and social spheres; fighting against women's poverty; and condemning all forms of violence against women. The distinction between sex and gender proved key to this political project—that is to say, the distinction between biological characteristics and social assignment (or presentation). The UN emphasized that social norms and patterns of behavior cannot be extrapolated from biological male- or femaleness and that these norms, in fact, evolve via socialization and upbringing.

Since then, legislators have written many equivalent laws, on a national and Europe-wide level. Through "Gender Mainstreaming," the European Union requires its member states to "mainstream" their practice in keeping with a specific perspective on sex-participation. This means they have to constantly consider whether policies might affect women and men differently. Many institutions started hiring permanent women's advocates and equal opportunities officers.

In the beginning, these jobs had been occupied by women with roots in the autonomous women's movements. Their ambition was to carry separatist-feminist politics into societies' institutions. But over time, it came to be bureaucrats and civil servants who took up these posts—women, and sometimes men, who didn't even necessarily see themselves as feminists.

LIBERATION, NOT EQUALIZATION

However, among feminists, there was a divided reaction to the institutionalization of feminist demands. Many rejected the idea that women could liberate themselves by means of "equalization" and adaptation to a male-dominated culture and its rules. Critics raised objections to the idea that a subject position based on unconditional solidarity between women—"We the Women"—even existed, from which one could level demands.

Among the first to contradict the universalizing claims of mainstream feminism was Audre Lorde, in a speech given to white academic women in 1984. Lorde demanded that her audience take the differences between women seriously, suggesting that difference, in itself, should become the starting point for feminist activism.

> *Our respective (nondominant) differences are interdependent.*

> *"Within that mutual interdependence lies that security which enables us to find true visions of our future. Difference is that raw and powerful connection from which our personal power is forged."*—Audre Lorde

In Europe, the pioneers of this nonessentialist "difference feminism" are the Italian feminists of the Women's Bookstore in Milan, and the "Diotima" community of women-philosophers in Verona. In 1989, in the book *How Feminist Freedom Arises*, the Milanese authorial collective postulates that the freedom of women stems from meaningful and strong relationships with other women. One of the most important exponents of this tendency is the philosopher Luisa Muraro (1940–).

"From the relationships among women and the liberation of our desire, we have learned of the existence of many strengths and potentialities that only need to be unleashed: powers that can help us to make the condition of womanhood freer, better and more pleasant. But then, the political parties, the Left, the state, and the European Union introduced this idea of 'equality' into feminism. Instead of women creating a new society, they made us believe that we have to take power."
—Luisa Muraro

Instead of investing themselves in a politics of demands (vis-à-vis the state, political establishment, and men), the Italian feminists proposed that women should share authority over their dreams and their projects exclusively with other women. This idea, known as "Affidamento" (confidence or entrustment), has become famous in Germany too.

QUEER FEMINISM

Simultaneously, many feminists began to fundamentally question the categories of "male" and "female" as well.

Oh, she's getting soaked!

Well, too bad. She's not a real woman.

No she isn't! You can't just buy your way into woman's identity with a few hormone tablets, after all.

Fine. Then I guess I'll just get an umbrella of my own.

. . . Then again, many did not.

The struggle in the 1960s that took place at the Stonewall Inn on Christopher Street in New York is widely acknowledged to be a seminal moment for queer politics. It was here that those excluded from the haunts of well-to-do gays and lesbians congregated: trans people, drag queens, LGBTI people of color, sex-workers, and homeless people.

It was they who were hit hardest by the violent raids that happened daily in the so-called "gay bars." Today, all around the world, events are held on "Christopher Street Day" to commemorate their resistance to this racist, transphobic, classist, and homophobic police violence.

In 1990 the influential book *Gender Trouble* was released, in which the philosopher Judith Butler (1956–) coined the term "heterosexual Matrix."

The term describes the assumption that there are precisely two unequivocally definable sexes, whose desires are mutually complementary.

People who did not want to conform to this binary sex logic adopted the term "queer"—which roughly means "strange, crazy, outside of every norm"—to describe themselves in a positive sense.

"'Biological sex' is an ideological construct that is coercively materialized over time. It is not a plain fact of the body, nor a static situation, but rather a process, by which regulatory norms materialize this 'biological sex,' and achieve this materialization by means of enforced and incessant repetition of these norms."
—Judith Butler

While, at first, it was above all lesbians and gays who called themselves "queer"—because they lived and loved outside the heterosexual norm— the word later became a collective term for the general diversity of sexual identities.

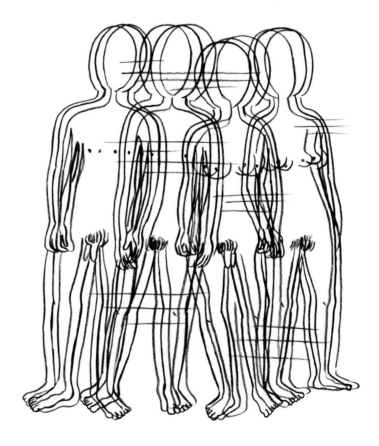

Today, the term "queer" encompasses inter-sexuality (which designates people who lack an unambiguous sex designation), transsexuality (people whose gender is different from the one that was assigned to them at birth), bisexuality (people who desire both men and women), and so on. To refer to all of these identities together there are acronyms such as LGBTQI (Lesbian Gay Bisexual Trans Queer Intersex)—a list that is by no means exhaustive, since new additions can always be made.

Originally wary of excluding people through its very acts of inclusion, the politics of "queer" has now become, more often than not, a label of identity.

THIRD-WAVE FEMINISM

So, since the women's movement in the 1980s was splitting off in various directions, it began to lose some of its cohesive power. At the same time, new countermovements appeared against feminism's achievements. Some men began countercampaigns aimed at safeguarding their privileges. The journalist Susan Faludi (1959–) analyzed this trend in her book *Backlash* in 1991. Meanwhile, some women considered feminism to be outdated because equal rights had been achieved; they called themselves "postfeminists."

Next, in opposition to these prevailing trends, a new movement began to form in the United States. It is sometimes called the "third wave."

The term comes from America. It goes back to a plea expressed by Rebecca Walker, the daughter (born in 1969) of the famous novelist Alice Walker.

In reaction to a court sentence acquitting a rapist, she wrote in 1992:

"I write this as a plea to all women, especially the women of my generation: Let this dismissal of a woman's experience move you to anger. Turn that outrage into political power. Do not vote for them unless they work for us. Do not have sex with them, do not break bread with them, do not nurture them if they don't prioritize our freedom to control our bodies and our lives. I am not a postfeminism feminist. I am the Third Wave."

Out of this movement, various projects developed that combined (for example) pop culture and feminism, like the "riot grrrls" and publications like *Missy Magazine* in Germany, which was launched in 2008.

REVOLUTION GIRL STYLE NOW!

riots not diets

SLUT

The division of feminism into separate "waves" is problematic in many respects. Within any of the groups designated as a "wave," people have promoted very different ideologies. Even so, there are several ways in which the themes of the third wave tend to distinguish themselves from the second. Third wavers reject the idea of a fundamental antagonism between women and men. They criticize any suggestion of "natural" femininity …

... and are skeptical of traditional forms of politics, favoring looser forms of organization and networking—for instance, via the internet.

They tend to feel comfortable in the realm of media and culture, where they react thoughtfully to every kind of dogma.

Urgh, that's still pretty sexist.

Yeah. Definitely. But who has the energy to stay mad all the time?

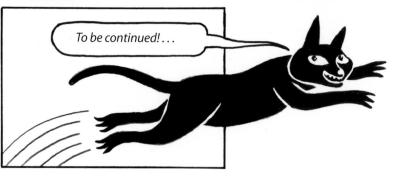

To be continued!...

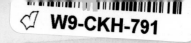

Mr. Whittier

Also by Elizabeth Gray Vining

THE TAKEN GIRL

(under the name Elizabeth Janet Gray)

I WILL ADVENTURE

SANDY

ADAM OF THE ROAD

THE FAIR ADVENTURE

PENN

MEGGY MACINTOSH

Truly thy friend

John G. Whittier.

Mr. Whittier

Elizabeth Gray Vining

THE VIKING PRESS   NEW YORK

FIRST EDITION

Copyright © 1974 by Elizabeth Gray Vining
All rights reserved
First published in 1974 by The Viking Press, Inc.
625 Madison Avenue, New York, N.Y. 10022
Published simultaneously in Canada by
The Macmillan Company of Canada Limited
Printed in U.S.A.

1   2   3   4   5   78   77   76   75   74

Library of Congress Cataloging in Publication Data

Vining, Elizabeth Gray, 1902–   Mr. Whittier.
Summary: A biography of the nineteenth-century Quaker
poet stressing his deep involvement in abolition, women's
suffrage, and other human rights, with emphasis on the
articles and poems he wrote in defense of his beliefs.
Bibliography: p.
1. Whittier, John Greenleaf, 1807–1892
—Biography—Juvenile literature. [1. Whittier,
John Greenleaf, 1807–1892. 2. Poets, American]   I. Title.
PS3281.V5   811'.3 [B] [92]   74–8162

ISBN 0–670–49431–3

Contents

Introduction

John Greenleaf Whittier at twenty-five took a courageous step that affected the whole course of his long life. He published at his own expense a pamphlet calling for the immediate abolition of slavery—and thereby opened himself to the hatred of thousands of people in the North as well as the South.

He was mobbed three times. He was condemned to poverty for many years. Although he liked women and was liked by them, he could not afford to marry. Well-known magazines would not publish his poetry. But through his editorship of abolitionist papers, his fiery poems against slavery, his astute political work as a founder and adviser of the Liberty Party (which supported antislavery candidates for Congress) he helped greatly to bring about the change of opinion that finally led to the freeing of slaves in the United States.

He realized earlier than most people that the Blacks in this country needed more than release from bondage: they needed also education, economic aid, and especially the respect for their humanity that is due to every human being.

He was passionately interested in freedom everywhere—in

Ireland, Poland, Italy, Brazil, Greece, Hungary, as well as in the United States—and he wrote poems about brave struggles for liberty in all those countries. He spoke out for women's suffrage and for coeducation in the universities. He respected craftsmen and distrusted machines. He saw that the new factories were setting up a different kind of slavery, in which wages were the master. He supported collective bargaining and the right to strike. He hated war.

After the Civil War was over, when he was nearly sixty, he came into his own as a poet. His great poem, *Snow-Bound: A Winter Idyll,* was immediately popular and was recognized as well-nigh perfect in its genre. *The Tent on the Beach* was a best seller. Better than any other American poet he has expressed the religious insights and aspirations of people of all denominations in words and rhythms simple, beautiful, and true. During the last twenty-five years of his life he was so widely known and greatly loved that his birthday was a school holiday in Massachusetts.

With the new century came a new kind of poetry, and for years Whittier was overlooked. Now that young people in the United States are again taking a stand on the very issues to which he gave his life and his pen—justice for Blacks, women, and workers; respect for individuals; Indian rights; disarmament—it is time to take a fresh look at Whittier. As the modern poet, Winfield Townley Scott, has written:

> *It is so much easier to forget than to have been*
> *Mr. Whittier.*

1. The Farm

Greenleaf's earliest poem was a bit of doggerel. It was written partly in fun, perhaps; all his life he had a way of saying in jest things that his heart felt seriously.

And must I always swing the flail
And help to fill the milking pail?
I wish to go away to school;
I do not wish to be a fool.

The flail was a long wooden handle with a shorter bar hinged to it and was used to beat the grain out of the stalk. It was too heavy for the tall, slender, delicate boy. His younger brother, Matthew Franklin, known in the family as Frank, was heavy-set and strong; he could swing the flail more easily. It was Frank who rescued the verse, which Greenleaf tossed aside, from being destroyed and forgotten.

Greenleaf's full name was John Greenleaf Whittier, but his family called him by the middle name. It was from his grandmother, Sarah Greenleaf, that he also got his French blood; the name originally was Feuillevert, translated literally as Greenleaf. Perhaps his large, deep-set, glowing dark eyes came from her too. Born on December 17, 1807, he was the second of four children. Mary, born in 1806, was the eldest. After Greenleaf came Frank, born in 1812, and Elizabeth, born in 1815. Besides the four children and their parents, the family included the father's brother, Uncle Moses Whittier, and the mother's sister, Aunt Mercy Hussey.

The sturdy old house in which they all lived had been built in 1688 by Thomas Whittier, the first of the family to come to America from England, and Whittiers had lived there ever since. It was situated in the northeastern part of Massachusetts near the New Hampshire border, fourteen miles from the ocean. When the wind was from the east the Whittiers could smell salt in the air and hear the surf rolling in on Salisbury Beach. It was a solid house with its great oaken beams and big central chimney, roomy enough to accommodate the family of eight and occasional visitors.

John Whittier, the father, was a man of standing in the community, a selectman of the town of Haverhill and a "weighty" member of the Quaker Meeting in Amesbury. Cousins came to stay from time to time. Important Quakers "traveling in the ministry" would stop with the Whittiers, and Friends on their way to the Yearly Meeting in Newport, Rhode Island, broke their journey at the farmhouse.

Downstairs to the right of the front door was the sitting room and to the left the parlor, which could also be used as a bedroom. It was here, in fact, that Greenleaf was born. Across the back of the house was the twenty-six-feet-long kitchen with its great hearth where all the cooking was done and where the family gathered on winter evenings to roast apples, drink cider, crack nuts, and tell stories. At one end of the kitchen was an old walnut desk, at which Greenleaf wrote some of his poems, and at the other the door into the small bedroom where the parents slept. Upstairs were four more bedrooms, which were not plastered. Sometimes in winter storms, when the wind shook the house, snow

The kitchen (*above*) and sitting room of the Whittier home in Haverhill

would sift in through cracks between the clapboards and drift across the beds.

The family were Quakers or, as they themselves would have said, members of the Religious Society of Friends. Their faith did not need the mediation of a minister or priest or the atmosphere of a church with a steeple, altar, candles, or sacred music; it depended directly upon the light within each heart. On Sundays, and usually in the middle of the week too, Friends met together in a plain meeting house and sat in expectant silence, waiting for the divine presence to be felt. Sometimes a Friend would be given a message to share with the others, and then he—or she, for men and women were equal—would rise and speak. Out of this experience came certain interior demands to be carried out through the week: simplicity of life, which avoided luxury; truthfulness of word and deed; obedience to conscience; respect for the divine light in others; and help to those who were in need.

The Whittier children probably did not learn very much in the nearby, one-room district school, for it ran only twelve weeks in each year. Some years the teacher was a good one, but usually he did not know much more than the pupils and spent most of his time keeping order with "birch and rule." But there were books at home—not many, perhaps thirty in all—that offered food for hungry minds. At fourteen Greenleaf made a catalogue of them in rhyme.

> The Bible towering o'er the rest,
> Of all the other books the best. . . .
>
> William Penn's laborious writing
> And a book 'gainst Christians fighting. . . .
>
> How Captain Riley and his crew
> Were on Sahara's desert threw. . . .
>
> The lives of Franklin and of Penn,
> Of Fox and Scott, all worthy men. . . .

The Scott mentioned was not Sir Walter the novelist but Job Scott, a Quaker who wrote of his religious experiences in his *Journal*.

Novels were not included in the home library. Not only Quakers, but people of other denominations too at that time considered fiction false and harmful. But Greenleaf managed to borrow a copy of Sir Walter Scott's *The Pirate,* recently published, and he and Mary read it together secretly at night. At the most exciting place his candle burned to its end and left them in the dark.

They were a close-knit, loving family, the Whittiers. John Whittier was a good farmer, a good father, a good man. When he was young he had made several trips on foot through the wilderness of northern New Hampshire into Canada with goods to trade; he liked to tell about his experiences. Abigail Hussey Whittier, Greenleaf's mother, was twenty-one years younger than her husband. She was a woman of dignity and serenity, with great dark eyes like her son's. Her hands were always busy with the spinning, knitting, sewing, and cooking necessary for her large family. Neighbors came to her for help when they had sickness in their homes. A reader, she knew many stories to tell when they sat around the fire in the evenings, stories of the Indians who lived near her girlhood home on the Piscataqua River, stories of witchcraft, legends of the sea, tales of Black children in Africa stolen away from their mothers and brought to America to be slaves.

Uncle Moses had been born on the farm and lived on it till he was killed when a tree he was cutting down fell on him. Greenleaf was seventeen when that happened; it was his first real grief. Moses Whittier knew nothing of books but everything, it seemed, about nature, about the weather, birds, fishing, the small animals of field and wood. He gave Greenleaf his first fishing pole. "But remember, boy," he said, "never brag of catching a fish until he is on dry land. I've seen older folks doing that in more ways than one and so making fools of themselves. It's no use to boast of anything until it's done, nor then either, for it speaks for itself."

Their much-loved Aunt Mercy, described by a friend as graceful and gracious, refined and playful, was unmarried. There was a romantic story about her. The man to whom she was engaged was away in New York seeking his fortune. Late one evening she saw him coming toward the farmhouse on horseback and riding past the window. She went to open the door for him, but when she got there she saw no one. She realized then that she had heard no hoofbeats. Several days later—for news traveled slowly in those days—she learned that just at the time she had seen him, he had died. This was a mystery that no one ever tried to explain; it was just accepted.

The youngest and the pet of all the family was Elizabeth, dark-eyed and olive-skinned like Greenleaf, gay and sweet. Like Greenleaf, too, she loved poetry.

The farm was a lonely one, the nearest house half a mile away. It lay on the eastern slope of Job's Hill, beside the road that led from Haverhill, three miles to the west, to Amesbury, nine miles to the east. Near the house was a bridge across the swift Country Brook, which was known as the haunted bridge. One night when Greenleaf was a small boy a woman came to their house in great fright, saying that she had seen a headless ghost on Country bridge. On a moonlit night soon after that, several boys went with Greenleaf to watch him make good his promise to run onto the bridge and call for the headless ghost. "Never shall I forget," he said many years later, "how my courage failed when in sight, but true to my promise I ran and shouted for the ghost to come forth, and immediately ran from the scene with all my might." A mile away was the Merrimack River, "broad and lovely" in Greenleaf's eyes, winding toward the sea. In the other direction was Kenoza Lake, about which clustered many legends.

There were sheep on the farm, oxen for plowing, seven cows to be milked, chickens, pigs, and bees for honey. Even though there was little money, there was always plenty of good food: chicken or ham or veal, apples and cider from the orchard, vegetables from the garden in front of the house, butternuts and chestnuts from their own trees. There was a horse to take them to Meeting in Amesbury; they had the only chaise in the countryside.

Each Sunday and Thursday the grown-ups at the farm drove to Meeting, with as many of the children as could be squeezed into the carriage. In winter it was bitterly cold. The parents had a theory that exposure to cold would harden a child and make him healthy, and so there were no lap robes. They had only short, tight jackets called spencers to wear over suits of loosely woven homespun, which let in the icy wind. The meeting-house itself, when they got there, had no stove. Greenleaf was glad when it was his turn to stay home, and in later years he thought that at least some of his ill health was caused by that early hardening process.

When Greenleaf was fourteen a book came into the house that had a deep influence on his life. The teacher at the district school that year was a young man named Joshua Coffin, a native of Newburyport and a student at Dartmouth College, whose studies had been interrupted by illness. After his recovery he taught for a term or two to earn money to return to college and get his degree. He was often at the Whittiers' house. One evening in front of the fire he read aloud from a volume of Robert Burns's poems, explaining as he went along the Scottish dialect.

Greenleaf was carried away with delight. Here was poetry more beautiful than anything he had read in the weekly newspaper that came to the house. In their own library there was no poetry at all, except a long dull poem by an old-time Quaker about the wars of the Israelites. Robert Burns, moreover, was a young man who had been a farm boy like Greenleaf himself, who saw beauty in the life around him and in the stories of his countryside and turned it into exquisite music. With sudden blazing insight Greenleaf saw that there was poetry in ordinary life, that his own country and his family were full of it, that even an unlettered boy could write verse that would speak to other hearts. Joshua Coffin, seeing Greenleaf's pleasure, left the book with him. Reading and rereading it, he began seriously to write poems himself, at first imitations of Burns and then poems of his own country.

The family doctor, Elias Weld, who lived in Rocks Village a few miles away, introduced Greenleaf to Milton. Weld had a small but good library, and he allowed Greenleaf to borrow from it. Like Abraham Lincoln, who was two years younger than he, Greenleaf often walked several miles to borrow a book.

He had one trip to Boston during his early years. In preparation for it he got a new homespun suit with "boughten" buttons and a hat made for him by his Aunt Mercy of drab velvet stretched over cardboard. Proudly he wore his new outfit to the great city. When he reached there he was astonished to see the crowds of people on the streets, each person intent on his own affairs. He had not imagined that there were so many people in the world. He drew back into an alleyway to let them pass and to catch his breath before venturing out again. No one even saw him. He might have been invisible. He began to be homesick. "It made no difference at all," he wrote later, "about my having those boughten buttons."

He had other experiences while he was in Boston. With some money that he had managed to save he bought a volume of Shakespeare. And, at the house of a cousin, he met a charming actress, who invited him to go to a play. But this he declined quickly, and he even went home earlier than he had intended because of it; his mother had warned him to have nothing to do with the theater.

By the time he was eighteen he had written a number of poems, which his sister Mary thought were every bit as good as the poems in the newspaper. Without telling him, she took one from the place in the attic where he hid his poems, copied it, and gave it to the carrier to take to the Newburyport *Free Press,* the four-page weekly newspaper that came to the farm. A few days later Greenleaf was working with his father mending the stone wall by the road when the carrier came riding past and tossed the newspaper over the wall. Greenleaf opened it casually, turning first as usual to the Poets' Corner. There he saw his own poem, "The Exile's Departure," signed "W., Haverhill, June 1, 1826."

In four stanzas of eight lines each, it told of the feelings of a young man about to leave Ireland to go and "dwell in a region unknown." The tide of immigrants from Ireland, though not so great as it was to be later in the century, was beginning to flow into New England. It was like Greenleaf, who loved his own home and the beauty of the country in which he grew up, to enter with imaginative sympathy into the feelings of one who had to leave his native land.

His father called him back to his work and he folded the paper and stuffed it into his pocket, but he could not help opening it from time to time to steal a look at his poem. On the page before the Poets' Corner he found a note: "If 'W.' at Haverhill will continue to favor us with pieces beautiful as the one inserted in our poetical department of today, we shall esteem it a favor."

Later in the same week the editor of the newspaper, accompanied by a young lady, drove out from Newburyport to see the poet for himself. He had learned where Greenleaf lived by questioning the carrier to whom Mary had entrusted the poem. When they arrived Greenleaf was crawling on his hands and knees in the dust under the barn trying to find the eggs of a hen who had stolen her nest. At first when Mary came breathlessly to tell him of the visitors from the town, he refused to see them, stricken with shyness and ashamed of the way he looked. But she persuaded him to go and change his clothes. He skirted around the back of the house, washed his face, and donned a clean pair of trousers, which, too late, he discovered were old and too short. Blushing and speechless, he presented himself in the parlor, where the editor and his friend were talking with Greenleaf's mother and with Mary. He saw a young man, slight, neat, well-mannered and friendly, whose silver-rimmed spectacles made him look like a country schoolteacher. The young editor, whose name was William Lloyd Garrison and who was actually only two years older than Greenleaf himself, put Greenleaf at his ease by praising his poems.

His father came into the parlor.

"Is this Friend Whittier?" said Mr. Garrison.

"Yes."

"We want to see you about your son."

"Why, what has the boy been doing?"

Garrison hastened to assure him that Greenleaf had been doing only good. He then went on to urge him to give his talented son further education.

Mr. Whittier replied that they were poor people and that he did not wish to have hopes aroused in his son that could not be fulfilled. "Poetry," he said with feeling, "will not give him *bread.*"

Garrison, who knew what it was to be poor himself, thought of Thomas Chatterton, the young English poet who had died of starvation in a garret, and he was silenced. Though he went away defeated, his visit had been important. It was the beginning of a friendship that was to have a far-reaching effect on Greenleaf's life.

Six months later, in January 1827, another editor came to plead with John Whittier to give his son more education. Abijah W. Thayer was the editor of the Haverhill *Gazette*, to which Greenleaf had sent poems after his initial success with the *Free Press*. Mr. Thayer came to Greenleaf's father with the news that an academy was going to open in Haverhill in the coming summer, and he urged him to send his son there. Greenleaf, he said, could board with the Thayers during the week and go home over the weekends.

2. The Academy

It was a kind—and a very attractive—offer. The problem was money. There was a mortgage of $600 on the farm, because at the time of their father's death John Whittier and his brother Moses had bought the shares that belonged to the other heirs. To pay the interest on the mortgage and the taxes took most of the cash that they received from the sale of farm produce. Moreover, since Moses Whittier's death, John Whittier needed Greenleaf's help to run the farm. He was willing, for the boy's sake, to get along without that, but he could not contribute anything to the expenses of tuition and board in Haverhill. Greenleaf would have to earn the necessary money himself. Tuition was $8 for a twenty-six-week term and $4 extra if Greenleaf wanted to take French—and he did. The regular rate for board was $1.50 to $1.75 a week.

The previous summer a hired man had earned extra money by making cheap slippers, and he offered to teach Greenleaf how to do it. Greenleaf now turned to and spent the winter making slippers. They sold for 25 cents apiece, but he received only 8 cents for each one. He calculated his expenses carefully, and he made just enough slippers to pay for everything and have 25 cents left over at the end of the term. So carefully had he figured and so strictly did he hold to his budget that at the end he had just exactly that.

Haverhill in 1827 was a village of three hundred buildings, of which four were brick. There were four churches, a circulating library, forty stores, including a bookstore, and three shipyards. Every day the stagecoach made the six-hour trip to Boston. The inhabitants were very proud of their new Academy, for which the land had been given by two sisters. A spacious and well-proportioned brick building, it had a cupola containing a bell, and it looked down from its height over open fields to the Merrimack River, the shipyards, the covered bridge, and the green hills on the opposite shore.

The Academy was dedicated on Sunday, April 30, 1827, with a formal ceremony. The procession marched from the First Parish Meeting House to the Academy, led by the headmaster, Oliver Carlton, and the Honorable Leverett Saltonstall of Salem, who made the principal address. Whittier had written an ode for the occasion, which was sung to the tune of "Pillar of Glory." "Hail, Star of Science!" the ode began, "Come forth in thy splendor. Illume these walls." It must be the only time that a school has opened with an ode written by one of the pupils. An elderly farmer named Robert Dinsmoor, who wrote in the Scottish dialect of his ancestors, also read a ballad.

The next day work began. There were four instructors, who among them taught a long list of subjects, including algebra, natural philosophy, rhetoric, surveying, Latin, French, and Greek, to thirty-nine boys and fifty-nine girls ranging in age from ten to twenty-five. One of them came all the way from New Orleans, several from Vermont and New Hampshire, the rest from Haverhill and nearby villages.

Greenleaf attended the Academy for two terms, 1827 and 1828. He paid for the second term by teaching at the Birch Meadow District School in West Amesbury. When he went before the school committee to apply for the job, they were so much impressed by his handwriting, which was small, neat, and legible, that they appointed him without going further into his qualifications—to his relief, for he was weak in mathematics. The older boys in the school soon found this out, and they took delight in bringing him difficult mathematical puzzles to solve. He had to take them home to work over them at night, but he was able always to bring back the solution in the morning, though at the cost of a sleepless night. And when his pupils were examined by the school committee at the end of the term, as the custom was, they did him credit.

These two terms at the Haverhill Academy were a time of growth and stimulation for Greenleaf, an opening out of his horizons far beyond anything he had so far known. The shy boy from the lonely farm found himself surrounded by lively young people, exposed to new knowledge and exciting ideas, and in contact with men and women of judgment and experience who took an interest in him. He considered his teacher, Oliver Carlton, "one of the best men—to use a phrase of *my craft*—that ever trod shoe leather." Mr. and Mrs. Thayer, at whose house he boarded, became lifelong friends. They were very fond of the handsome, intelligent young man with his courtesy, his quick wit and his strong feeling for truth and justice, and they helped him wherever they could, then and later.

Nearly every week Mr. Thayer printed one of Greenleaf's poems in the *Gazette,* usually signed Adrian or Donald. Many of Donald's poems were written in Scottish dialect, like Robert Dinsmoor's, of which they were an imitation. Many had come out of his reading, as the titles show: "The Death of Ossian," "The Grecian Women," "The Massacre at St. Bartholomew," and "The Sicilian Vespers." None of them was very good, and he was never willing to have them included in his collected works, but they attracted favorable attention at the time. The *Saturday Evening Post* of Philadelphia reprinted one without giving credit to its author. The editor of the *Boston Statesman* commented that it was remarkable that the poetry of one "occupied in manual occupations" should show a capacity usually acquired only by "a study of the best models." Actually Whittier had read a great deal of Scott and Byron, and imitating them was a detriment rather than a help toward finding his own style.

During the winter before Greenleaf's second term at the Academy, when he was teaching school at Birch Meadow, Mr. Thayer proposed to publish a volume of his verse to be called *The Poems of Adrian*. It was announced in January in the *Gazette* with a flattering description. "It is believed that these poems indicate genius of a high order, which deserves all possible culture." The purpose of publishing the poems, it was stated, was to help the author to obtain a classical education. They were to be printed on two hundred pages of the best paper, bound in boards, to sell for seventy-five cents. Unless five hundred copies were subscribed for by March 1 the book would not be published. A news item in the same issue reported that twenty-two subscriptions had already come from Philadelphia.

For two more weeks the book was advertised, but after that there was nothing more about it. March 1 came and went in silence. Evidently not enough people were interested in it to warrant its publication. Though it may have been exciting to Greenleaf to see his work so highly praised, this experience evidently convinced him that his father had been right when he said, "Poetry will not bring him *bread*." He continued to write it, nevertheless, and by the end of the year had come out from his disguise and was signing his poems J. G. Whittier or John G. Whittier.

He was welcome, too, in the house of Judge and Mrs. Minot, who opened to him their fine library. Their son George, who was ten, and their twelve-year-old daughter, Harriet, were also pupils at the Academy. George, who considered Greenleaf "the best of all the big fellows" in the school, called him "Uncle

Toby." Judge Minot liked to discuss politics with him. Harriet, reminiscing in later years, remembered that "he was a very handsome, distinguished-looking young man. His eyes were remarkably beautiful. . . . With intimate friends he talked a great deal and in a wonderfully interesting manner; usually earnest, often analytical and frequently playful. He had a great deal of wit. . . . When any wrong was to be righted or an evil to be remedied, he was readier to act than any young man I ever knew and was very wise in his action—shrewd, sensible, practical. . . . He was very modest, never conceited, never egotistic. One could never flatter him. He did not flatter but told very wholesome and unpalatable truths, yet in a way to spare one's self-love by admitting a doubt whether he was in earnest or not."

He was popular with the other boys and girls and made many friends with whom he kept in touch long afterward. He was especially interested in two of the girls, Evelina Bray and Mary Emerson Smith.

Evelina Bray from Marblehead, who was at the Academy in 1827, was the first to whom he gave his susceptible heart. She said in old age that she had been engaged to Whittier and that he broke it off because she was not a Friend. It is doubtful if they were really engaged, for he was only nineteen and had his way to make in the world. It is easy for a woman to imagine in later years that there had been an engagement when actually there was only some sweet talk in the moonlight. It is certain, however, that Greenleaf felt that he could not marry anyone who was not a Friend. The Society of Friends in the nineteenth century was strangely narrow. Members who "married out of Meeting" were expelled unless they declared publicly that they repented—and what loyal and spirited young man or girl in love is willing to do that? His religion went deep with Whittier. Though he might humorously declare his horror at the thought of having to marry a Quaker girl in a "bonnet like a flour dipper and a face as long as a

A Quaker family. Women did not wear the bonnets
that looked like "flour dippers" indoors

tobacco yawl," he was not willing to give up a way of worship that so richly fed his spirit as the expectant silence of the Quaker Meeting did. He had many a discussion with his girl friends about Quakerism and Calvinism, which he thought a "stern creed."

Mary Emerson Smith was a second cousin. She was staying in Haverhill with her grandparents. Captain Nehemiah Emerson had fought in the Revolution, and his wife, the former Mary Whittier, was a first cousin of Greenleaf's father; Greenleaf called her "Aunt Mary." But Mary Emerson Smith was not a Quaker either, and her parents, who lived in Dover, New Hampshire, moved in more worldly circles than the Whittiers. Mary was fifteen when she came to the Academy, a pretty girl with curly brown hair and hazel eyes, gay, candid, friendly, interested in dancing and the latest fashions. Greenleaf looked up to her for her knowledge of "verbs and nouns and philosophy and botany and mineralogy and French and all that" and because "she had seen something of society and could talk (an accomplishment at the time to which I could lay no claim)." They went walking together in the moonlight along the Merrimack; they talked about many things, from Calvinism to beards; she teased him about his whiskers, and he teased her about her interest in fashions and her many beaus, but there was a deeper undercurrent in his feeling for her.

In the autumn of 1828, after two terms, he had finished with the Academy. He would soon be twenty-one. He must decide what direction his life would take: the farm, teaching, further education, what?

3. Editor

The only ways to earn money that Greenleaf knew were by making cheap slippers and teaching school. He put shoemaking aside with a joke, and his experience in the district school had given him a permanent distaste for teaching. Farming he knew, for he had been trained by his father and his uncle, but this rugged life demanded a physical strength that he did not have. Today the natural solution for such a boy would be further education, and for one of his intelligence and capacity for hard work, a scholarship would be forthcoming from somewhere.

In his time there were no scholarship funds. His book of poems had come to nothing. The only possibilities of getting the money for tuition were borrowing it, with a burdensome debt to pay later, or asking some rich friend to give it to him, and his independent spirit rebelled at that. In a letter to Abijah Thayer in November 1828, before his twenty-first birthday, he explained how he felt.

"I have renounced college for the good reason that I have no disposition to humble myself to meanness for an education—crowding myself through college upon the charities of others and leaving it with a debt or obligation to weigh down my spirit like an incubus and paralyze every exertion.''

He thought that the professions were already overcrowded, and he saw his ''miserable knack of rhyming'' as no good to him, for though his poems were widely published not one was paid for. Another opportunity, however, appeared through his friend, William Lloyd Garrison.

After six months with the Newburyport *Free Press,* Garrison had gone to Boston to edit a temperance newspaper called the *National Philanthropist,* and from there to Bennington, Vermont, to edit still another newspaper, in which he could promote not only temperance but the abolition of slavery and of war. He arranged for Whittier to be offered his position on the *Philanthropist.*

The publisher was a Baptist minister named William Collier, who with his son published two weekly newspapers and a monthly magazine and kept a boarding house on Federal Street in Boston. One of his newspapers was the *National Philanthropist;* the other was the *American Manufacturer.* In the end it was the editorship of the *American Manufacturer* that was offered to Whittier, with a salary of nine dollars a week and free board with the Colliers.

So, just turned twenty-one, John Greenleaf Whittier went to Boston to begin his first editorial job. The purpose of the paper was to promote American manufactures and protective tariff and to support Henry Clay, the senator from Kentucky who favored native industry. Up until now New England's prosperity had come from its farmers and merchants, but mills were being built along the swift streams where there was good water power, and a whole new economy was developing.

Though Whittier was much more interested in temperance, emancipation, and peace than he was in industry, he stayed for seven months with the *American Manufacturer.* During that time he saved money from his small salary to contribute toward paying off the mortgage on the farm. He learned a great deal about printing as well as about editing. He published some of his poems. He read widely in the excellent Boston libraries. He enjoyed going to the Athenaeum Gallery to look at the paintings—and at the pretty girls who also frequented the place. "I always did love a pretty girl," he wrote to a friend. "Heaven grant there is no harm in it." With all of this activity, he was lonely. He did not find the Colliers congenial, and he thought Boston had, as he wrote to Mary Emerson Smith, now in a seminary at Kennebunk, Maine, "a coldness and a formal sort of politeness which disgusts me. I cannot love this city."

His correspondence with Mary, of which only six of his letters and none of hers survive, began in May 1829 after he had written and torn up many letters to her. "Mary," he wrote, "I have loved you passionately, deeply—and you, if there is any faith in 'women's words'—*you* have not *hated* me. Do you remember the last talk we had on the banks of the Merrimack when the moon of autumn was looking down on us? Ay, and a hundred others— they are living in my memory."

Evidently in her reply she offered to be a sister to him, a well-worn way of turning a man down, for in his next letter he thanked her for allowing him to consider her as a sister. Love, he said, which ends in matrimony, he placed "out of the question. And yet it sometimes seems to me that the most perfect happiness obtainable on earth results from the married state. But alas for me! I have had dreadful forebodings of my destiny." He pictured himself perched on the "high seat" in Meeting with his Quaker intended beside him wearing the kind of bonnet he disliked. "Such must be my lot unless, indeed, I come to the conclusion to lead a life of 'single blessedness.' "

A later letter he began, "My dear sister" and signed, "Your affectionate brother." "I know of no one," he said in this letter, "who occupies so large a share of my thoughts. . . . You know not the intensity of my feelings. . . . You said something about the impropriety of a lady's holding correspondence with a gentleman. Dismiss the idea. It is unworthy of your noble spirit. Is a woman to be kept down by the influence of an unjust fashion forever? Has she no innate feeling of pride and security which would enable her to hold converse with the arrogant 'lords of creation'?''

It was part of his Quaker inheritance that he thought of a woman as a person in her own right, not to be hampered by meaningless conventions. From the beginnings of Quakerism women had been free to speak in the Meetings for worship and to take part in the business of the Society. It was on the other hand not characteristic of him to call her "you" instead of "thee." All of his life he used the "plain language" with everyone.

After this letter there is a gap of three years before the next one. Mary went to live with an uncle in Cincinnati; perhaps in the interest and novelty of her life there she failed to keep Whittier's letters.

He had not forgotten Evelina Bray. During the summer there was a Quarterly Meeting at Salem, to which Greenleaf went with his mother. Early one morning he walked over to Marblehead, two or three miles away, to call on Evelina. It was too early for her to invite him into the house, and so they walked together to the old fort, where they sat on a ruined wall looking over the harbor, talking. Three years later she was graduated from the Ipswich Seminary for Female Teachers and after that went off to teach in various Southern and Midwestern cities. She did not marry till 1849.

He went back to the farm in August, partly in order to help his father, who was not well, and partly because he was "dissatisfied" with the *American Manufacturer*. Later in the year Abijah Thayer moved to Philadelphia to start a new paper there, the *Commercial Advertiser,* and Whittier succeeded him as editor of the *Essex Gazette,* for which he could do most of the work at home.

There were at that time a great many small local newspapers. Some of them lasted only a short time, but they had an influence much greater than their size or stability. In a day when there was no radio or television, no telephone or telegraph system, they were the only means by which people learned about what was happening in the state legislature, the U.S. Congress, and, to a lesser degree, the world beyond. Almost everybody subscribed to them and those who did not borrowed them from others. Their poetry was read, their news discussed; they had weight in politics.

By the time that Whittier came to the *Essex Gazette,* William Lloyd Garrison was in Baltimore editing, along with a Quaker abolitionist named Benjamin Lundy, a paper devoted entirely to the antislavery cause, the *Genius of Universal Emancipation.* In April 1830 Garrison was accused of libel by a notoriously cruel slave trader and was thrown into jail. Whittier wrote in the *Gazette* that he would rather share his friend's cell than live in the proudest home in the South. It was perhaps more an impulsive declaration of sympathy than the result of reasoned thought, but it shows the way his mind was turning. He also wrote to Henry Clay asking him to intervene, but before the senator could take action a New York Quaker had paid Garrison's fine and he was released.

Whittier's father died on June 11, 1830, at the age of sixty-eight. Very soon after that an unexpected and flattering offer came to Whittier to edit the *New England Review* for six months during the absence of its editor, George Prentice, who had been asked to take time off and go to Kentucky to write a campaign biography of Henry Clay. The election of 1832 was looming ahead, and Clay was expected to run against Andrew Jackson. The *Review,* published in Hartford, Connecticut, was a political paper which supported Clay. Whittier had sent poems and essays to it, and Prentice had printed them. He and Whittier had become friends through correspondence, though they had never met.

The salary was small, $500 a year, but the job offered an opportunity to see more of the country and to meet influential people, especially politicians, and Whittier was becoming more and more interested in politics. He preferred Clay to Jackson, for though Clay, like Jackson, was a slave owner, yet he was a man of peace, and Jackson was a general, whose Indian policy Whittier disliked. He hesitated to accept Prentice's offer because he was not sure that he ought to leave the farm at that time, but his mother encouraged him to take it. He went to Hartford in July.

George Prentice, five years older than Whittier, was a man of another world, strong, lively, well-dressed, a good talker with a gift for satire. The leaders of Hartford were surprised when they walked into Prentice's office and saw Whittier sitting at his desk, a shy young man of twenty-two straight from the farm in a home-spun suit of Quaker cut. But he was also handsome, with his mop of black hair, his sideburns, which were a new and rather daring style at the time, and glowing dark eyes, and he had considerable charm. His lively wit and his vigorous and fresh ideas, as well as his genuine friendliness, his industry, and high sense of duty soon won their respect.

The Hartford experience, though it lasted little more than a year altogether, was important for Whittier in the process of finding himself and the path in life that was distinctly his own. In Boston he had been in a small backwater of Baptists and reforming interests; in Hartford he was out in a larger world.

The *New England Review* was widely read and as its editor he met many of its well-known contributors, persons who shared his interest in literature and politicians who had influence. He was fortunate in being able to board in the house of Jonathan Law, a former postmaster, a scholarly man who had a fine library. Mrs. Lydia Sigourney, later to be known as "the sweet singer of Hartford," was beginning to publish her sentimental poems in magazines and newspapers, and she welcomed the young poet to her house. Another friend was Frederick C. Barnard, eighteen months younger than Greenleaf, who was a teacher at the Institute for the Deaf and Dumb. Later he became president of Columbia University, and Barnard College was named for him. In a long poem called "Miriam," which Whittier wrote many years later, he tells how he and Barnard "in youth and hope" drew their horoscopes "thick-studded with all favoring stars." He was much attracted by a girl named Cornelia Russ, but not only was she not a Quaker, but she was beyond his reach by reason of her wealth and social position.

As he became more expert in handling his newspaper, Whittier had time for writing of his own. In February 1831 he published his first book, a small volume called *Legends of New England,* containing eleven stories in verse and seven in prose, most of which he had rather casually collected from Essex County tales or from the books of Increase and Cotton Mather, New England preachers and writers of the seventeenth century. Years later he was ashamed of it, and he bought up all the copies he could find, once paying five dollars for one, and burned them. He said the book "seemed like somebody else." But he was among the first to show interest in the native legends, which have since become a field of scholarship in themselves. Even the word "folklore" had not been invented then. Longfellow and Hawthorne were still unknown. Longfellow at twenty-four was a professor and librarian at Bowdoin College. Hawthorne, three years older, was leading a lonely life in Salem, Massachusetts, writing short stories that he could not get published. For some time to come American poets would be writing on European subjects and imitating European styles.

In the *Review*, as well as supporting Henry Clay, Whittier began to write articles against slavery. He hailed the appearance of the *Liberator*, Garrison's great new paper devoted to the cause of abolition. In his first issue Garrison uttered a declaration of his intentions that was a ringing call to courage: "I am in earnest—I will not equivocate—I will not excuse—I will not retreat a single inch—AND I WILL BE HEARD." From the first the *Liberator* aroused violent opposition. Many threats were made against Garrison's life. It took courage even to praise the *Liberator* as Whittier did.

NEW-ENGLAND WEEKLY

VOL. III. HARTFORD, CON. MONDAY, JULY 26, 1830.

NEW-ENGLAND WEEKLY REVIEW,
PUBLISHED EVERY MONDAY BY
HANMER & PHELPS,
Office in the New Exchange Buildings, north of the State-House.

J. G WHITTIER, EDITOR.

TERMS.—To subscribers in the city, and to single subscribers by mail, $2 per annum, in advance. No paper discontinued until all arrearages are paid. A liberal discount made to companies. Advertisements inserted on the usual terms.

*** All Letters on business relating to the Office should be addressed to the Publishers, post paid.

THE REVIEW.

THE FORSAKEN GIRL.

"They parted—as all lovers part—
She with her wronged and broken heart;—
But he, rejoicing he is free,
Bounds like the captive from his chain:
And wilfully believing she
Hath found her liberty again."
L. E. Landon.

If there is any act which deserves deep and bitter condemnation, it is that of trifling with the inestimable gift of woman's affection. The female heart may be compared to a delicate harp—over which the breathings of early affection wander, until each tender chord is awakened to tones of ineffable sweetness. It is the music of the soul which is thus called forth—a music sweeter than the fall of fountains or the song of Houri in the Moslem's Paradise. But wo for the delicate fashioning of that harp if a change pass over the love which first called forth its hidden harmonies.—Let neglect and cold unkindness sweep over its delicate strings, and they will break one after another—slowly perhaps—but surely. Unvisited and unrequited by the light of love, the soul-like melody will be hushed in the stricken bosom—like the mysterious harmony of the Egyptian Statue, before the coming of the sunrise.

I have been wandering among the graves—the lonely and solemn graves. I love at times to do so. I feel a melancholy not unallied to pleasure in communing with the resting place of those who have gone before me—to go forth alone among the thronged tombstones, rising from every grassy undulation like the ghostly sentinels of the departed. And when I kneel above the narrow mansion of one whom I have known and loved in life, I feel a strange assurance that the spirit of the sleeper is near me—a viewless and ministering angel. It is a beautiful philosophy, which has found its way unsought for and mysteriously into the silence of my heart—and if it be only a dream—the unreal imagery of fancy—I pray God, that I may never awaken from the beautiful delusion.

I have been this evening by the grave of Emily. It has a plain white tombstone, half hidden by flowers, and you may read its mournful epitaph in the clear moonlight, which falls upon it like the smile of an Angel, through an opening in the drooping branches. Emily was a beautiful girl—the fairest of our village maidens. I think I see her now, as she looked when the loved one—the idol of her affections, was near her with his smile of conscious triumph and exulting love. She had then seen but eighteen summers, and her whole being seemed woven of the dream of her first passion. The object of her love was a proud and wayward being—whose haughty spirit never relaxed from its habitual sternness, save when he found himself in the presence of the young and beautiful creature, who had trusted her all on the 'venture of her vow,' and who loved him with the confiding earnestness of a pure and devoted heart. Nature had deprived with a strong heart to mingle with the world—girded with pride and impelled forward by ambition. He found the world cold, and callous, and selfish, and his own spirit insensibly took the hue of those around him. He shut his eyes upon the past—it was too pure and mildly beautiful for the sterner gaze of his manhood. He forgot the passion of his boyhood—all beautiful and holy as it was—he turned not back to the young and lovely and devoted girl, who had poured out to him in the confiding earnestness of woman's confidence the wealth of her affection. He came not back to fulfil the vow which he had plighted.

Slowly and painfully the knowledge of her lover's infidelity came over the sensitive heart of Emily. She sought for a time to shut out the horrible suspicion from her mind—she half doubted the evidence of her own senses—she could not believe that he was a traitor—for her memory had treasured every token of his affection—every impassioned word and every endearing smile of his tenderness. But the truth came at last—the doubtful spectre which had long haunted her; and from which she had turned away, as if it were sin to look upon it, now stood before her a dreadful and unescapable vision of reality. There was one burst of passionate tears—the over-flow of that fountain of affliction which quenches the last ray of hope in the desolate bosom,—and she was calm—for the struggle was over, and she gazed steadily and with the awful confidence of one whose hopes are not of Earth, upon the dark Valley of Death, whose shadow was already around her.

It was a beautiful evening of Summer, that I saw her for the last time. The sun was just setting behind a long line of blue and undulating hills, touching their tall summits with a radiance like the halo which circles the dazzling brow of an Angel—and all Nature had put on the rich garniture of greenness and blossom. As I approached the quiet and secluded dwelling of the once happy Emily—I found the door of the little parlour thrown open, and a female voice of a sweetness, which could hardly be said to belong to Earth, stole out upon the soft Summer air. It was like the breathing of an Æolian lute to the gentlest visitation of the Zephyr. Involuntarily I paused to listen—and these words—I shall never forget them—came upon my ear like the low and melancholy music, which we sometimes hear in dreams:—

"Oh—no—I do not fear to die
For Hope and Faith are bold,
And Life is but a weariness—
And Earth is strangely cold—
In view of Death's pale solitude
My spirit hath not mourned—
'Tis kinder than forgotten love,
Or friendship unreturned!

And I could pass the shadowed land
In rapture all the while—
If one who now is far away
Were near me with his smile.
It seems a dreary thing to die
Forgotten and alone—
Unheeded by our dearest love—
The smiles and tears of one!

Oh! plant my grave with pleasant flowers,
The fairest of the fair—
The very flowers he loved to twine
At twilight in my hair.—
Perchance he yet may visit them,
And shed above my bier
The holiest dew of funeral flowers—
Affection's kindly tear!"

It was the voice of Emily—it was her last song. She was leaning on the sofa as

For the New-England Weekly Review.

THE FAREWELL.

Farewell;—I feel that thou and I,
Must part even now, perhaps forever.
I heard last night thy long good bye
And chained, but with a proud endeavo
The smothered tide of tearful feeling—
I could not bear that other eyes
Should smile upon the heart's unsealing
Of all its hidden sympathies.
Oh—was it not a mocking thing
At that last hour of parting sadness
Over the fount of tears to fling
The light and careless smile of gladness;

Yes—sadder eyes were fixed on thee—
And sadder tones bespoke regret:
And trembling hands were proffered free,
And young, fair cheeks with tears were wet
And I—the saddest one of all—
Returned thy greeting with a smile—
That smile was for the crowded hall—
My *heart* was with thee all the while,
And burning thoughts were thronging there—
The hopes and fears affection hath
To prompt its still, unuttered prayer
For blessings on the loved one's path.

They tell me thou wilt choose thee one
Of brighter eyes and glossier curls—
Among the "children of the sun"—
The silver-toned Italian girls:
That she will love thee with the glow
And joy of her voluptuous clime;
And whisper music, like the flow
Of soft winds in the summer time:—
That when the moonlight sleepeth on
Gay Venice and her many isles—
And when the gondalier alone
May mark the dalliance hour of smiles
Thy arm will bear her yielding form—
Thy hand amid her tresses play,
And fervent kisses, soft and warm,
Disturb at times her melting lay.

Alas!—I would believe thee true—
And yet I fear a change will come
And waste away, like morning dew,
Affection's rich and untold sum.
For thou wilt roam in other lands,
And other eyes will smile on thee,
And thou wilt ask from other hands,
The gifts which I have proffered thee
For I have seen thee in my dream
Of feverish and unquiet sleeping,
Devoid of all which man should seem
When Love around his path is weeping
I've seen thee at the altar-side,
And listened to the rites which gave
Unto thy arms another bride,
And left forsaken love—a grave!

God grant my dreams may never prove
Their stern reality of wrong;
Nor make the meaning of thy love
A ring—a promise—and a song.
I do believe thou lovest me now—
But will thy boyish dream remain,
When foreign suns have lent thy brow
A darker and a manlier stain?
And wilt thou love my memory, while
Above thee bends th' Italian sky?
Or where the Grecian maidens smile—
Or where the Georgian dance goes by?

Farewell!—forgive the doubts which fling
A shadow on our parting hour,—
Nor deem my heart a wayward thing—
A jealous and ungentle dower:
For woman's love is blent with fears—
Her confidence—a trembling one—
Her smile—the harbinger of tears—
Her hope—the change of April's sun
Farewell!—and oh! where'er thou art,
Indulge at times a thought of me,
And I will sooth my trembling heart
In one long dream of love and thee.

J. G. W.

(From the Harbinger of Peace.)

CAUSE OF PEACE.

Many there are, doubtless, who will exclaim, "How fruitless are all attempts to promote concord amongst men, the human heart is, and ever will be, the slave of the formation," who would have dared to hail him as the harbinger of that glorious dawn which now opens on our view? that general diffusion of gospel light which now irradiates the world, and pierces the gloom of "the dark places of the earth, the habitations of cruelty?" When Howard visited the pestilential prisons of Europe, how would it have animated his heart, to have known that the patronage of power, the influence of the nobility, the talents of the wise, and the sympathies of the female sex, were soon to be exerted in behalf of that cause, in which he was a solitary laborer! And if there be one case which is more apposite than another, it is the change of opinion in favor of humanity, which has taken place on the subject of the Slave Trade. What would now be thought of such language as the following, in reference to Africans who had been thrown overboard alive: "The matter left to the Jury was, whether it was from necessity; for they could have no doubt, though it shocked him very much, that the case of slaves was the same as if horses had been thrown overboard."* Few persons at the present time could be conceived so far to have abandoned the common feelings of humanity, to be so deeply biassed by prejudice, or so debased by avarice, as to make such an observation. Yet this, only forty years ago, was the language of one of the greatest lawyers of the day, in a court of justice and in a case where 140 innocent human beings were destroyed for the purpose of fraud.

These instances show that the labors of those who toiled at first almost without hope, have been crowned with success, far greater than they could have supposed possible: and while they throw around those who now labor, an enlivening gleam which exhilarates their hopes, they prompt them to unwearied and persevering activity.—"Our enemies are lively, and they are strong," far more powerful and more numerous than one who have ever been challenged to the combat. Those who unfolded the horrors of the Slave Trade, opposed the interests of comparatively few persons whilst those who endeavor to place War in its true character, run counter to the sentiments of almost every individual. From the monarch to his meanest subject; from the greatest scholar to the peasant, whose mind is scarcely less expanded than the beast he drives; through all ranks and professions, in all countries and kingdoms, one sentiment has prevailed, and that is, that war is lawful and honorable. Thousands look to its continuance as their only employment, their only road to honor and emolument. With all the energy and talent that were displayed, and all the influence and activity that were exerted, aided too, by the frequently repeated and warm expressions of the people, it required no fewer than twenty years after its cruelties were fully organized, to stamp the mark of criminality upon the Slave Trade. Can it then be expected that a Society which is as yet in its infancy, unaided by any powerful auxiliaries, should in the short space of a few years be able to interpose and put a stop to the devastating band of war!—Those who anticipate effects so important, from causes so inadequate, should recollect not only the extent, but the inveteracy of the disease. Such a change of opinion as is necessary to annihilate war, is not to be expected in so short a time. It was not the anticipation of the Peace Society that they should thus speedily produce a change in opinions so desirable; their object was to diffuse information tending to show that war was an unchristian, inhuman, and unjust method of settling national disputes. If, by the statement of undisputed facts, and by clear and irrefragible arguments, they have been able to strip war of its meretricious splendour; if by an appeal to the humanity, justice, and religious principles of the christian world, they have in some degree excited their attention to a subject of such importance; if they have thrown before the world a body of evidence, and a collection of arguments, on the subject of war, entirely unprecedented—then, whatever objects may retard their progress, we are bound to acknowledge that they have made no inconsiderable advance toward the accomplishment of their purpose.—This through the blessing of Providence they have effected.

The little stream which to the casual observer appears lost amidst the mountains of opposition, supplied from that spring whose resources are unfailing, is secretly and silently pursuing its course, and while the eye retraces its various meanderings,

At the end of the six months George Prentice did not return to resume his place on the *Review*; he was offered a better job in Kentucky. Whittier expected to stay on as editor in Hartford, but in March 1831, after he had been editing the *Review* for seven months, he was called home to settle his father's estate, and there he was taken ill. He had always been delicate, but now the state of his health began to dominate his life. Severe migraine headaches, neuralgia, and palpitations of the heart were to plague him for as long as he lived and often incapacitated him entirely. The rest of that year he spent going back and forth between the farm and Hartford, and in January 1832 his name disappeared from the masthead of the *Review*.

At home, cared for by his mother and his younger sister, pacing his activities to suit his strength, he again edited the Essex *Gazette*, worked on the farm, wrote poetry—and dreamed of a career in politics. He was surprisingly unrealistic about it, for if he was not strong enough to edit a city newspaper, how could he endure the still more arduous life of a politician, with its strenuous campaigns for election and its pressures to compromise? But he recognized politics as the way in which reforms are put into the actual life of a country, and he had a talent for political strategy. "What an absurdity," he wrote in one of his editorials, "is moral action without political action!"

He thought of moving to Cincinnati to edit a newspaper there. After referring to a letter from her, he wrote to Mary Emerson Smith in August 1832, "Six months ago I really considered myself a citizen of Cincinnati. I had determined upon going to the West. I anticipated a great deal of happiness and sooth to say in all my bright dreams a certain fair friend of mine and certain old but treasured associations and recollections flitted past my vision." His ill health had again intervened.

It was a long letter. He wrote of his political interests and of the plan that his friends had of his running for election to the House of Representatives in order to break a long deadlock in which neither of two candidates had been able to win a majority. Still only twenty-four, he was too young to run and there was no way to hold up the election until after his twenty-fifth birthday in December. He gave her news of their classmates at the Academy, and he referred to a criticism that had been made of Mary herself.

"You have been censured by some for your openness and candor, for your natural cheerfulness in the presence of your friends, for your unstinted disclosures of the emotions of your heart. I have ever considered them as among the most beautiful and engaging traits of your character and yet I cannot but own that they may be liable to misconstruction. Excuse this serious part of my letter. 'Tis a Quaker sermon and you will put up with it for the sake of its oddity." Later in the letter he said, "What is that thing I hear about a medical friend of yours? Guilty or not Guilty? 'Tis said you are positively engaged off there. . . . O Mary, you are the cruelest girl I ever knew to go for to break a body's heart with as little remorse as if you had only broken your shoestring."

The letters to Mary were long and interesting, sometimes playful, always warm and affectionate. She kept them, she hardly knew why. When she was an old lady and Whittier was dead, she said, "I always revered Whittier. I don't know that I ever loved him any better than I do now. What youth of twenty or twenty-one in these days would write such letters of wisdom and humor, so full of a pure love without passion or prejudice as were those after he left school? Why I kept them I know not. I did not read them for nearly forty years. I knew he was unlike other young men but I was surprised at the beauty of his life."

A month after he had written to Mary he was writing to Jonathan Law, his Hartford friend.

"I have done with poetry and literature. I can *live* as a farmer and that is all I ask at present. I wish you could make me a visit, you and Mrs. Law; our situation is romantic enough—out of the din and bustle of the village, with a long range of green hills stretching away to the river; a brook goes brawling at their feet, overshadowed with trees, through which the white walls of our house are just visible. In truth, I am as comfortable as one can well be, always excepting ill health."

But actually he was not quite so placidly contented as he sounds in this letter. Consciously or unconsciously he was aware of his own potential strength and talent and he was looking for an outlet, and for something more exciting—fame. He had written to George Prentice, "I am haunted by an ambition, perhaps a very foolish desire of distinction, of applause, of fame, or what the world calls immortality."

His last letter to Mary was written on March 3, 1833. Evidently she had asked his opinion of the waltz, a dance then rather new and considered daring. "On the whole," he answered, "if I were a dancer I know I should passionately love the waltz." But he was a Quaker. He told her that Haverhill was "fearfully dull" that season. "Now and then we have a temperance lecture or by way of variety and amusement an occasional meeting of the Tract Society. Now, Mary, if you should against nature, probabilities and reason, happen to be an old maid, don't be a *tract-distributing* one. I shall expect to hear you give an account of the conquests you have made and the hearts you have broken. And I, in return, will give you my own history since I saw you and detail all my love adventures. I think that by thus comparing notes we could afford each other some amusement. Don't you?"

There were no more letters. She was married that year to a young lawyer of Cincinnati.

Those months at the end of 1832 and the beginning of 1833 must have been dark ones for the restless young man in love with an unattainable girl, ambitious to play a part in the world, eager to win fame. It was a time of uncertainty and frustration as well as of searching, but soon he was to find his way clear to make a commitment from which he would not turn back. Sometimes all other roads must be blocked before the seeking soul discovers the one that is really his own.

4. Justice and Expediency

For more than a year Whittier had not heard from his friend Garrison, though he had written to him. Garrison was too busy writing, printing, and mailing the *Liberator* to write letters. But in March 1833 Harriet Minot and two friends of hers wrote a fan letter to him, signed "Inquirers after Truth." He replied in part, "You excite my curiosity and interest still more by informing me that my dearly beloved Whittier is a *friend* and townsman of yours. Can we not induce him to devote his brilliant genius more to the advancement of our cause and kindred enterprises and less to the creations of romance and fancy and the disturbing incidents of political strife?"

Later in the month Garrison wrote to Whittier himself, urging him to enter actively into the struggle against slavery. "Whittier, enlist! Your talents, zeal, influence, all are needed." Soon after that Garrison was proposing a trip to Haverhill to make an address there on slavery. Whittier found him a church in which to hold his meeting. The weekend was successful, and the friendship between Whittier and Garrison was strengthened. Whittier wrote a poem about Garrison which he later published in the Essex *Gazette*. It began:

Champion of those who groan beneath
  Oppression's iron hand:
In view of penury, hate and death
  I see thee stand.

Even more important, Whittier's already warm interest in the cause of abolition had been heated to the boiling point. Soon after this meeting Garrison left on a trip to England, and Whittier decided to write the manifesto that proved to be the turning point in his life.

It was not Garrison's influence alone that brought this about. Whittier did not need to be convinced that slavery was wrong. His Quaker heritage had set him against it from his earliest childhood. The first organized protest in the world against slavery had been made by German Quakers in Philadelphia in 1688. John Woolman, Anthony Benezet, and others had given their lives to persuading Friends to free their slaves, with the result that from 1777 on no Quaker held slaves. Whittier's love of freedom arose also from his reading of Milton's *Areopagitica*, a ringing appeal for freedom of speech, and of the poems of Byron, who died in the cause of Greek independence. "When freedom is threatened anywhere in the world," Whittier wrote once, "it is threatened everywhere." He had already written articles against slavery in the various newspapers he had edited, but this meeting with Garrison brought him to the point of committing his own life to the cause.

He spent the next two months in studying the subject, gathering his material, collecting quotations from Plato to James Monroe. In May, sitting at his great-grandfather's walnut desk in the farmhouse kitchen, he wrote at white heat a paper calling for the immediate abolition of slavery. This was at that time not only a revolutionary, but a dangerous subject to handle. It was not poetic exaggeration that made Whittier see Garrison faced with poverty, hatred, and physical danger; abolitionists were mobbed, imprisoned, stoned, detested.

He attacked first the moral evil of slavery. Then he showed the inadequacy of schemes other than emancipation for getting rid of it. Gradual abolition he dismissed with scorn, comparing it to "gradually refraining from robbery, lust and murder."

Once, Whittier pointed out, Virginia planters like Washington and Jefferson had denounced slavery and looked forward to eliminating it. Now, with the rice and cotton fields of the far South calling for more and more slave labor, it was profitable in Virginia to breed Blacks in order to sell them. Textile manufacturers in the North needed the cooperation of the cotton growers, and so they supported slavery. Instead of being gradually abolished, it was spreading into new states.

He took up the popular scheme of colonization, by which free Negroes were to be helped to emigrate to Africa, there to establish a new country of their own, Liberia. The American Colonization Society, of which Henry Clay was president, had been widely approved in both North and South, and churches had taken up collections for it. Even Whittier and Garrison had been in favor of it earlier, but in the second issue of the *Liberator* Garrison had come out with an article exposing the flaws in the scheme. Now Whittier made a still more powerful attack on its weaknesses and inconsistencies. Only free Negroes were eligible. Since 1817 only 613 Negroes had been sent, at great cost, to Africa, while the number of slaves in the United States had increased by 550,000. Also, the society made clear that it had no objection to slavery itself, and it opposed the education of Blacks in the United States.

Whittier marshaled facts and figures to show that free labor was more efficient and therefore more profitable than slave labor. Justice, he pointed out, was actually more expedient than injustice. From this argument came the title of his pamphlet, *Justice and Expediency or, Slavery Considered with a View to its Rightful and Effectual Remedy, ABOLITION.*

He called for the immediate abolition of slavery in the District of Columbia and the territories of Arkansas and Florida, to be

THE LIBERATOR.

VOL. I.]   WILLIAM LLOYD GARRISON AND ISAAC KNAPP, PUBLISHERS.   [NO. 24.

Boston, Massachusetts.]   OUR COUNTRY IS THE WORLD—OUR COUNTRYMEN ARE MANKIND.   [Saturday, June 11, 1831.

followed by all of the slaveholding states. This he would bring about not by force, but by the overwhelming moral conviction of the nation. He pointed out that it had been in this way that the importation of slaves had been stopped.

It was a closely argued, eloquent piece of work for a young man of twenty-five and a courageous attack on an institution not only supported by the majority of the people of the United States at that time but implicitly permitted in the Constitution.

When the essay was written he was faced by the question of getting it before people. It was too long, twenty-three pages, to print in the Essex *Gazette* or any other weekly newspaper. It was too short for a book, and in any case no commercial publisher would touch it. He decided to print it as a pamphlet at his own expense.

And now as the first excitement of composition died down he began to count the cost. Not only would the printing charge take a large bite out of his small earnings for the year, but the unpopularity that would result from it would be sure to affect his life for many years to come. He knew well that he was entering upon a long struggle. Slavery would not be abolished in a year or two, and once he had started on this path there would be no turning back. He could not look forward to editorial jobs in better known and better paying newspapers. His poems would not be welcomed in national magazines. Political office would be closed to him. Even his life might be in danger. All of these risks Whittier faced, and then he had his pamphlet printed and sent it out to newspapers and prominent people.

The response was electric. The pamphlet was discussed. It was denounced. It was copied. Moses Brown, a rich Quaker of Providence, Rhode Island, arranged for the *Providence Journal* to reprint it. The *Anti-Slavery Reporter* devoted its second issue to it. Arthur Tappan, a New York Quaker, had five thousand copies printed and distributed. A Richmond, Virginia, paper, the *Jeffer-*

sonian, made a bitter attack on it. It caused, to Whittier's distress, the death of a good man. Dr. Reuben Crandall, of Washington, D.C., was so moved that he passed it along to a friend to read. Very soon he found himself in prison on the charge of disseminating subversive literature. Conditions in the jail were so bad that his health broke down; shortly after he was acquitted and released he died.

It sometimes happens to a young person that he cannot see clearly what his life should be. He is distracted by many possibilities and influences. He wavers and changes course many times. Then something happens: he makes a decision to do one perhaps simple thing, and after that all doors close except that one which opens upon the single path that is his own destiny to follow. His personality becomes integrated, the meaning of his life clear. This is what happened to Whittier. For the next thirty years, until slavery was finally abolished, he gave himself to the cause of emancipation. He put aside his dreams of success and fame to enter upon this difficult, demanding, and occasionally dangerous course. As Professor Edward Wagenknecht has said, "He took his place with the outcasts, and he knew exactly what he was doing."

He never regretted it.

5. Conventions and Mobs

One of the early results of *Justice and Expediency*, Whittier felt, was his losing by one vote the nomination to the Massachusetts legislature. He was now too well known as an abolitionist. Another result was that the Boston Young Men's Association selected him to be their delegate to a convention to be held in Philadelphia to establish an American Anti-Slavery Society. He wrote to William Lloyd Garrison that he could not afford the trip. "As thee knows our farming business does not put much money into our pockets." A generous Boston abolitionist named Samuel E. Sewall, however, came to the rescue with the necessary funds, and at the end of November Whittier and Garrison set out by stagecoach for New York. There they were joined by his old schoolteacher, Joshua Coffin, who was now secretary of the New England Anti-Slavery Society, which had been formed a year earlier, and by the Reverend Samuel J. May. May, young and in Whittier's words "sunny-faced," was an ardent abolitionist, a Unitarian minister, and an uncle of Louisa May Alcott, who had been born in Germantown, Pennsylvania, a year earlier. From New York they all went on to Philadelphia, reaching there on December 3.

This was Whittier's first visit to the Quaker city, which he was later to know well. He saw very little of it at this time, for during the three days that he spent there he was engrossed by the convention.

It opened on December 4, 1833, in the Adelphi Hotel on Fifth Street below Walnut, and Whittier was elected one of the two secretaries, the other being Lewis Tappan, the brother of Arthur Tappan. They had to hold their meetings in the daytime because the mayor of the city declared that the police could not protect them at night. The cause of abolition was unpopular in Philadelphia, where there were many textile manufacturers dependent on cotton raised by slave labor in the South and increasing numbers of Irish immigrants who resented the competition of free Negroes, of whom there were forty-eight thousand in the city.

Even the Quakers, who had actually initiated the struggle against slavery more than a century earlier, were not united on the abolition movement. Their commercial interests and their fear of war caused them to prefer the safer plan of gradual emancipation. Those among them who were abolitionists gave themselves wholeheartedly to the cause, risking fines and imprisonment for their part in the Underground Railroad, a secret organization that helped fugitive slaves.

Of the sixty-two delegates who came to the convention from New England, New York, New Jersey, Pennsylvania, and Ohio, twenty-one were Quakers and all were men. Two or three were Negroes. A few women attended some of the sessions as guests, and Lucretia Mott spoke eloquently at one of them. Lucretia Mott, a Quaker from Nantucket, had come with her husband, James, to live in Philadelphia, where he was in business. A slender, feminine, able, and beautiful woman, the mother of six children, she was active in the cause of abolition and other reforms including, later, women's rights. She and James Mott entertained many well-known visitors in their spacious house on North Ninth Street.

Lucretia Mott

The convention rather quickly drew up a constitution, but it believed that it also needed some more stirring statement of its aims and purposes. Accordingly it appointed a committee of three, Whittier, Garrison, and May, to draft a Declaration of Sentiments. This powerful and radical document, written largely by Garrison, called for immediate emancipation, to be achieved peacefully, beginning with the abolition of slavery in the District of Columbia and the territories of Florida and Arkansas and with the ending of the slave trade between the states.

On the last day of the convention, December 6, the declaration, beautifully inscribed on parchment (like the Declaration of Independence), was solemnly read by Samuel May. Then one by one as their names were called—beginning with the delegate from Maine, who was also the oldest member—the delegates rose, went forward, and signed their names in silence. Not all the delegates took this step. Only half signed it. It was felt to be a serious and important act, committing all who took part to a lifetime of struggle. The document was subsequently called the Declaration of Independence of the Negro in America. Thirty years later Whittier said of it, "I set a higher value on my name as appended to the Anti-Slavery Declaration of 1833 than on the title-page of any book."

J. Miller McKim, a young Presbyterian minister, thought that Whittier in his frock coat and standing collar, with his sideburns and his dark flashing eyes, looked more military than Quaker. "His broad square forehead and well-cut features, aided by his incipient reputation as a poet," he wrote, "made him quite a noticeable figure of the Convention." Gone were the old homespun clothes of the farm boy. Whittier had become, in a Quaker way, something of a dandy. His suits were conservatively cut by a good tailor and made of fine broadcloth. He had his boots made by a French bootmaker, and when the man later returned to France, Whittier sent to Paris for his boots. He never wore the Quaker broad-brimmed hat but the fashionable stovepipe instead and in winter a sealskin cap.

In the following year Whittier wrote one of the most famous of his antislavery poems, which became known under the title, "Expostulation." It began:

> *Our fellow countrymen in chains!*
> *Slaves in a land of light and law!*
> *Slaves crouching on the very plains*
> *Where rolled the storm of Freedom's war!*

The poem had a compelling rhythm and a passion of feeling that made it very moving to the people of the time. It was published in the *Liberator* and was immediately widely copied, quoted, recited, and reprinted in a broadside with an emotion-arousing picture of a kneeling Negro with chains at his wrists and ankles. Garrison hailed it as "a blast that shall ring from Maine to the Rocky Mountains."

Though his poetry attracted attention, only one of Whittier's poems—a "Lament" for an older friend who had died—brought him a small fee, from the *New England Review*. Throughout 1834 he worked on the farm with his brother Frank and continued to write poems, articles, and letters, which were published in weekly newspapers. In clear, vigorous, and persuasive prose he advocated the abolition of slavery by both moral and political action; he urged the Congress to abolish slavery in the District of Columbia and the territories and to end the domestic slave trade. He believed that slavery, thus confined, would ultimately wither away in the slave states. He believed in the usefulness of sending petitions on these issues to members of Congress, for they aroused debate, which was reported and discussed all over the country. He ran again for the state legislature of Massachusetts, and this time he was elected representative from North Essex.

In December an English abolitionist named George Thompson arrived in this country, having been invited by Garrison to come for a three-year speaking tour. After only a little over a year he had to be smuggled out of the country to save his life. Thompson was thirty years old, tall and slender, a powerful and attractive speaker, who had played a part in England's abolition of slavery in all her colonies. A rumor, quite unfounded, quickly went around New England: he had come for the purpose of stirring up ill feeling between the North and South for the benefit of English manufactures. His message, unpopular in itself, was further resented as foreign interference in America's domestic affairs. When he spoke in January at Andover, Massachusetts, he was pelted with rotten eggs. As the months went on his speeches everywhere were the signal for disturbances.

Besides the New England manufacturers, who wanted Southern cotton, the churches of New England were indignant with the abolitionists for a quite different reason. They had gone all out for the Colonization Society, believing that it would not only bring about the gradual freeing of the slaves, but even more important would lead to the conversion to Christianity of the Africans when American Christian Negroes went to live among them. When Whittier and Garrison and others denounced the Colonization Society as the "handmaid of slavery," the churches were outraged. The angry mobs that attacked Thompson—and with him, Whittier—were inflamed by misplaced patriotism (believing Thompson to be an English agitator), by a selfish interest in slavery, and by what they thought was religious fervor. Many of them, of course, simply enjoyed the excitement of a fight for its own sake. Though they seldom carried guns, there was real danger from stones, from tar and feathers, and sometimes even the threat of lynching.

In the late summer of 1834 Thompson, with threats against his life, came to seek safety at the farmhouse with the Whittiers.

He and Samuel May arrived together. May was to speak in a church in Haverhill, and Thompson and Whittier were going together to Plymouth, New Hampshire. They got there safely and Thompson delivered three lectures, which went off without incident. On their way back they stopped at the house of a man named George Kent in Concord, where a meeting had been planned in the courthouse in the evening.

When the hour drew near, a mob gathered, and the selectmen of the town ordered the courthouse to be closed. Thereupon the mob set off for George Kent's house in search of Thompson. Before they reached it, they met Whittier with the editor of the local newspaper, and mistaking Whittier for Thompson, they pounced on him. Rotten eggs ruined Whittier's suit, and stones crashed against the wooden fence behind his head. Fortunately he was hit only in the leg, but it was enough to lame him for a time afterward. For all his life he was to remember the sound of those stones banging against the fence beside him. He and his friend were near the house of a brother of Kent's, who opened his door and pulled them inside. The crowd of men and boys went to the State House Park, where, having had some drinks on the way, they made a dummy figure of George Thompson and burned it, firing a triumphant cannon.

While this was going on Whittier quietly went to George Kent's house, where he and Thompson spent the night. They got little sleep, for the mob came back and kept up an uproar outside the windows from two o'clock until first daylight. While they were still shouting and firing off rifles in front of the house, a horse and carriage were brought to the side door, and Whittier and Thompson got in. Someone swung the gate open for them, and they drove furiously through the astonished crowd and galloped out of town over the Hookset bridge, which was the only one unguarded.

When they stopped at an inn for breakfast they heard the landlord telling some rough-looking men a lurid story about the previous Sunday night at Haverhill. The foreigner, Thompson, they said, and the dangerous Quaker abolitionist, Whittier, had been beaten up. They had escaped into New Hampshire but handbills had been printed—and he showed them one—calling for the capture of Thompson.

"How is the rascal to be recognized?" inquired Whittier.

"Easily enough. He's a tongue-y fellow."

The dangerous Quaker and the tongue-y fellow finished their breakfast composedly and then, when they were safely in the carriage again, Whittier leaned out and called to the landlord, "This is George Thompson and my name is Whittier." Off they went, before the landlord recovered from his surprise.

What had really happened at Haverhill the Sunday evening before was bad enough. It was Samuel May who had spoken in the Christian Church, after the First Parish Meeting House had been denied him. The room was filled with convinced abolitionists who listened attentively until a stone crashed through the window, scattering pieces of glass among the congregation. It was followed by larger stones, and a cannon was drawn up before the door. The meeting was hastily adjourned.

When Samuel May came through the threatening crowd, Elizabeth Whittier on one side and Harriet Minot on the other linked arms with him, and the three walked steadily forward. The two girls were well known and respected in Haverhill, and nobody would harm them. They passed in safety to the Minots' house. Elizabeth, when she wrote up the incident in her diary, modestly made no mention of her own and Harriet's brave action. "The lecturer," she wrote, "went quietly to the home of his kind friend Minot."

After their return from Concord, New Hampshire, Thompson spent a quiet week at the farmhouse, raking hay and speaking at a prayer meeting at the district schoolhouse nearby. The day after Thompson left, Whittier went to Boston to "recommence," as Elizabeth wrote, "his legislative duties."

At a boardinghouse in Franklin Street he roomed with Robert Rantoul, Jr., the representative from Gloucester. He was a young lawyer, a graduate of Andover and Harvard, who like Whittier opposed slavery and capital punishment. Two years later Rantoul was to go to the U.S. Congress. In the Massachusetts legislature Whittier made no speeches, but he attended the sessions conscientiously, served on two committees, and learned much about politics. The following year he was re-elected, but his doctor forbade him to serve on the grounds of ill health.

While Whittier was in Boston Garrison spoke at a meeting of the Female Anti-Slavery Society. The mob broke in and, dragging him out, put a rope around his neck and hauled him along the street toward, they shouted, the gallows. Whittier, at a session of the legislature, heard the uproar in the street outside. Knowing that Elizabeth was at the antislavery meeting, he hurried out to take care of her if necessary. He saw Garrison being rescued and taken to the Leavett Street jail for protection. As soon as he had made sure that all the women had got away uninjured, he and Samuel May went to the jail to visit and comfort Garrison.

Two years later Whittier had another encounter with a mob, this time in Newburyport, where he had gone to hear Henry B. Stanton speak to the Essex County Anti-Slavery Convention. The meeting was broken up by the shrill sound of fish-horns, the clashing of tin pans, and human howls. When rotten eggs and sticks began to fly through the air, Whittier and his companion, an elderly minister, departed "at an undignified trot." When they stopped to catch their breaths, Whittier said to the clergyman, "I am surprised that we should be disturbed in a quiet Puritan city like Newburyport. I've lived near it for years and thought it was a pious city." The minister answered, "Young man, when you are as old as I am, you will understand that it is easier to be pious than it is to be good."

He was to have one more—and a much more dangerous—experience of mob action in Philadelphia three years later. He did

Garrison in the hands of the Boston mob

not fear injury but he did dread the ignominy of tarring and feathering. The victim was stripped, plunged into melted tar, and then a feather bed was ripped open and shaken over him. After that, to the sound of jeers, he was perched on a rail and carried out of town. One of Whittier's later poems would describe such an event, "Skipper Ireson's Ride," the recounting of an old legend in which a hardhearted skipper who refused to stop to rescue sailors from a skinking ship was tarred and feathered on his return home by the furious wives and mothers of the lost men.

> *Poor Skipper Ireson, for his hard heart*
> *Tarred and feathered and carried in a cart*
> *By the women of Marblehead.*

It was one of his best ballads.

In 1836 Whittier was again editing the Essex *Gazette,* advocating freedom of speech and of the press, in defiance of the governor of Massachusetts, who had asked the people of the state not to discuss slavery and had even suggested a law against abolitionists. When many of the *Gazette'*s readers, agreeing with the governor, objected to Whittier's views, he was demoted to junior editor in charge of poetry and literature. He quietly resigned.

About this time the old farmhouse was sold. Greenleaf was not strong enough to work the farm, and Frank had married and moved to Dover, New Hampshire. With the money from the farm Whittier bought a small house in Amesbury across the street from the Friends' meeting house and moved into it in July with his mother, his Aunt Mercy, and Elizabeth. It was a one-story house with a large garden behind it where there were a grape arbor and a pear orchard. There were four rooms downstairs and one in the attic. They added a small room at the southwest corner for Aunt Mercy. The move was especially difficult for Elizabeth.

"I have been here now five weeks," she wrote in her diary, "and save my brothers and sister have seen but five of my Haverhill friends and certainly those five seem dearer than ever. I wonder if I shall ever love Amesbury or its people!"

Greenleaf's other sister, Mary, was by this time married to Jacob Caldwell and lived in Haverhill with her husband and two children.

Whittier published his first book devoted wholly to poetry this year, a tiny volume of sixty-nine pages no more than four inches square, entitled *Mogg Megone*. It was a long poem dealing with the murder of a Saco Indian chief, which had been published in two issues of the *New England Magazine* the year before. It received a favorable notice in the *North American Review*, but Whittier was later to regret it and to try, without much success, to suppress it. Looking back on it fifty years later he said, "It suggests the idea of a big Indian in war paint strutting about in Sir Walter Scott's plaid."

He also wrote several antislavery poems. One was addressed to the daughters of James Forten, a leading Negro of Philadelphia and a friend of Whittier's. It began, "Sisters! the vain and proud may pass you by." A dark poem based on an actual incident told the story of a slave ship on which a dreadful disease spreading from the slaves in the crowded hold to the crew above came into port with no one alive but its captain. He wrote also a compassionate hymn for a meeting of the Anti-Slavery Society in New York, which began:

> *O Thou whose presence went before*
> *Our fathers in their weary way.*

It is still sung in part in churches today.

Though he was no longer in the Massachusetts legislature, he was not done with politics. He believed always that change came through political means, and he continued for many years to be active behind the scenes. He was indefatigable in gathering signatures for petitions calling for the abolition of slavery in the District of Columbia and of the slave trade between the states. He supported the re-election of Caleb Cushing to the U.S. Congress three times, for as long as he kept his promise to support the right of petition, and he skillfully mapped much of the strategy of political campaigns in Massachusetts.

He set out for Washington in January 1837 to see John Quincy Adams, Caleb Cushing, and Robert Rantoul in action. When he got as far as Philadelphia he learned that Congress was debating what became known as the "Gag Rule," cutting off all petitions to Congress and limiting discussion on the slavery question. Changing his plans, he attended an antislavery convention in Harrisburg, where he met Governor Joseph Ritner, a farmer of Pennsylvania Dutch ancestry, who stood firmly for freedom. On his return to Amesbury Whittier wrote a poem, "Ritner," in which he praised the governor for his untrammeled spirit.

He was looking for another editorial job, and in the spring an offer seemed likely to come from Portland, Maine, where a group of abolitionists planned to start a weekly newspaper with Whittier as editor at a salary of $1,200. He hesitated to accept it because he feared the harsh climate of Maine and also because he thought there would be more action in Pennsylvania. But as it turned out, 1837 was a depression year and the scheme fell through because of financial difficulties.

He went to the Yearly Meeting of Friends in Newport in June and from there to New York, where for about two months he was one of the secretaries of the American Anti-Slavery Society.

6. Action
in Philadelphia

He boarded in Brooklyn at the house of Don F. del Floys, a Spaniard, whose English wife had a brother dedicated to the abolitionist cause. "I see all the French and Spanish ladies in the city," he wrote to Harriet Minot.

He also saw an American girl, Lucy Hooper, who was twenty years old. He had met her in Newburyport before her family had moved to Brooklyn two years earlier, where her father was a merchant. The family were not Quakers but Episcopalians. Like many another susceptible young girl she had been greatly taken with the handsome poet and was disappointed when he paid her little attention. A year earlier she had confided in a friend, "In truth I did wish to have been in Haverhill with you and to have seen H. Minot and John Greenleaf Whittier, whom I am glad you have seen for now you can understand my admiration of him. . . . I fear he has forgotten me, but I hope not."

Now they met again when he was a stranger in Brooklyn, and she and her family welcomed him to their house. She had a small talent for writing poems, a number of which had been published, and she asked Greenleaf's advice about collecting them in a volume. He encouraged her but advised her to wait until she had written something longer. ''The truth is,'' he wrote to her, ''the 'small craft' of poetry in which we have indulged ourselves is not fitted for the voyage of Immortality.'' After some reflections on time and fame he asked, ''Why not write a poem on which we can concentrate all our powers? I have long thought of doing this myself, but I have nearly abandoned the idea. An accumulating pressure of other matters compels me to forego the undertaking. But what should hinder thee from doing it? Nothing that I can conceive of.'' After some remarks about a poem by a ''Massachusetts lady'' which he sent her, he assured her that he thought she could write a long poem ''which would be received with general commendation on both sides of the Atlantic.'' Unfortunately he did not have time to take the walk with her that had been proposed.

His work in New York was not very arduous. The Anti-Slavery Society had several secretaries, and he shared an office on Nassau Street with some of them. One was Henry B. Stanton, who had had all the buttons cut off his coat when he made a speech in Newburyport—at the same meeting from which Whittier had fled in company with the wise old minister—and another was Theodore D. Weld, a gentle but determined abolitionist who had many Black friends. Still another was James G. Birney, a lawyer from Kentucky, who had freed his own slaves and come to New York to work for abolition; he was the oldest of the group, fifteen years older than Whittier. He and Weld once went up on the balcony of City Hall about nine in the evening and talked until nearly sunrise.

The secretaries edited two antislavery papers, the *Emancipator* and the *Anti-Slavery Review,* sent letters and petitions to congressmen, arranged for lectures and meetings, wrote pamphlets, and took part in the Underground Railroad. All this activity was financed by several rich New Yorkers and by Joseph Sturge, an English Quaker who was later to have an important part in Whittier's life.

Because of his old trouble with palpitation of the heart Whittier did not keep regular hours but took the ferry over from Brooklyn when he felt well enough. Even so the pace of the city was too swift for him, and near the end of August he left for Boston and home. He wrote to Lucy, "My health has suffered from my residence in New York—a place which, with all due deference to thyself, I must consider unfit for Christian, or heathen even, to dwell in."

While he was in New York a Boston publisher, Isaac Knapp, issued a small volume of ninety-six pages, *Poems Written during the Progress of the Abolition Question in the United States between the Years 1830 and 1838. By John G. Whittier.* He had not consulted Whittier nor given him a chance to choose or to edit the poems, of which there were twenty by Greenleaf and one by Elizabeth Whittier. He was paid nothing for his poems.

The call to Philadelphia came late in the fall. Benjamin Lundy, whom he had first met at Collier's boardinghouse ten years earlier, had been publishing an antislavery weekly in Philadelphia called the *National Enquirer*. Lundy was a Quaker saddlemaker who had sold his shop and devoted his money and his life to the fight against slavery; he published newspapers, started antislavery societies, made speeches and went about the country on foot, talking to people and trying to convince them. He had walked from Baltimore to Bennington, Vermont, to ask Garrison to come to Baltimore to work with him on the *Genius of Universal Emancipation*. An attack on Lundy on a street in Baltimore by a slave trader and Garrison's term in prison had brought the *Genius* to an end. Now, tired and ill, Lundy was asking for Whittier's help. He was only forty-eight in years, but his life had been exhausting and he was an old man.

Although Philadelphia was no longer Penn's green country town, still it was an attractive city between its two rivers, the Delaware and the Schuylkill, with lines of red brick houses shaded by linden and horse-chestnut trees. It had a modern waterworks at

Fairmount on the Schuylkill; a horse car ran the length of Chestnut Street; there were railway trains to Germantown, to Baltimore, and to Reading; and steamboats plied the Delaware.

Whittier already had friends there. His cousins, the Wendells, lived on South Sixth Street. Joshua Coffin, his old schoolmaster, was there, taking part in the Underground Railroad. Abijah Thayer was editing the *Commercial Herald.* At first Whittier stayed with the Thayers, but soon he went to board with Joseph and Rachel Healy on North Seventh Street. Joseph was a printer and printed most of the antislavery books and pamphlets in the city; he was also the financial agent for the Pennsylvania Anti-Slavery Society. Other young people boarded in his house too: Sarah Lewis, a year and a half older than Whittier, who with her friend Sarah Pugh had a school for girls on Cherry Street; and Benjamin Jones, who was younger, who had a bookstore on Arch Street, where he sold abolition literature. It was a convenient and friendly place to live, though the cook was a notoriously poor one, and Whittier moreover missed his New England squash pie and pork and beans.

An enterprise that interested all of the antislavery people in Philadelphia was the building of Pennsylvania Hall at North Sixth Street and Haines Alley, a little more than a block from the Healy house. The abolitionists had no place in the city in which to hold large meetings, for no public hall dared to have them and the churches, always conservative, refused. Even the Friends' Meetings declined. Many Quakers were ardent abolitionists, but the leaders of the Society in Philadelphia were timid and, according to Whittier, "lukewarm."

"Their ancient and excellent testimony against slavery," he wrote scathingly in the *Pennsylvania Freeman,* "has been in too many instances sacrified to prejudice, mercantile connexions with slaveholders and a somewhat inconsistent dread of association with other sects for any other purposes than worldly gain."

Determined to make themselves heard, the antislavery people of all denominations gathered together to build a hall of their own. They raised the money by selling subscriptions for twenty dollars each, and they planned to pay off the shareholders by renting out the auditorium and lecture room and offices to other liberal groups. The response was good. Many of the shares were bought by workingmen, by women and by free Blacks. By the time Whittier arrived in Philadelphia, the walls were rising.

The abolition movement had had a bad setback during January of that year when the Pennsylvania legislature passed an amendment to the state constitution limiting the vote to white men. Up until then free Negroes in Pennsylvania had voted as a matter of course, but from 1838 to the Civil War no Black man was to cast a vote in that state.

Philadelphia had many solid, self-respecting Black citizens, some of them well-to-do. They had businesses of their own, such as sail-making, catering, and building; they were active in the Underground Railroad; some of them were charter members of the Abolition Society—even though in the white churches and Quaker meeting houses they were still confined to the back benches. Only the Roman Catholic churches let them sit where they pleased.

During this winter Whittier was involved briefly with the Underground Railroad, which had recently been organized under the leadership of a Committee of Twelve, who directed the activities of many other members. Two market women in Baltimore, one white and one Black, helped by furnishing certificates of freedom for slaves to use. James Forten, a rich Black sailmaker who had a house on Lombard Street, and his son-in-law James Purvis, who had a place in Bucks County, provided shelter for escapees in both places. Groups of women met in Philadelphia houses to make clothes for the fugitives, who often arrived wearing the single burlap garment that was allowed to many slaves. Some were put on the Reading Railroad and sent North, others taken to Arch Street Wharf at midnight and put aboard Captain Whilden's boat to be taken on to Bordentown and from there by train to New York.

Edwin Coates, who was one of the Committee of Twelve, told a story of Whittier's involvement, which is quoted in Samuel T. Pickard's *Life and Letters of John Greenleaf Whittier*.

Like all of us he learned that the great secret of our success was to be cautious, discerning and *never to make a mistake*. A mistake, a blunder, meant the penitentiary and years of painful imprisonment. A Virginia slave named Douglas applied to the committee for help to get his wife and children into a free state. We dispatched an agent to Baltimore to consult with the vigilance committee there, and finally a letter was sent to the family by an efficient female agent by the name of Butler who worked her plans and ours so well that in a short time the little party landed in Philadelphia.

At eleven o'clock that night there came to my house a consequential-looking individual who handed me a copy of the Washington *Globe* at the same time pointing to an advertisement containing a reward for the recovery of the runaways and a full description of each one. As may well be imagined, I began to grow alarmed. So as soon as this person had withdrawn, I started for the residence of Whittier, and was closeted with him for an hour. A conviction for complicity meant personal injury, or at least imprisonment for a long and indefinite term. Without coming to any conclusion as to the best course to pursue I went home and to bed. I know I kept looking at the penitentiary with one eye and on the God of the oppressed with the other. But it providentially turned out all right, and I had the unspeakable pleasure of soon meeting with the family in a secure place and shaking hands with them all. I then with joy rushed to Whittier's house, at the still hour of midnight, and called my anxious friend out of bed. From the room below I called,

"Whittier! Whittier! the Douglas family is safe!"
From his chamber came the exclamation: "Glory! Hallelujah!"—and this is the first time I remember hearing a
Quaker shout. But he did, and it came from his very soul.
We soon had barbers and dressmakers and others to assist
in changing the personal appearance and effecting a complete disguise of the determined slaves, and when they left
that house, with their wigs, strange clothes, and other
changes, they could not have been recognized as the same
party who entered it.

In March Benjamin Lundy retired altogether from the *National Enquirer* and left it to Whittier. Since it was now to be
published as the organ of the Pennsylvania Anti-Slavery Society,
he changed its name to the *Pennsylvania Freeman*. He designed a
plainer and smaller masthead than Lundy had had and broke up the
solid pages into shorter and more attractive-looking articles, but he
made few other changes. The four-page, eight-columned, closely
printed paper was made up of reports of Anti-Slavery Society
meetings all over the North, accounts of legislation dealing with
slavery, stories of the ill-treatment of slaves or the achievements of
free Negroes, letters, long quotations from other newspapers, news
items including reports of injustices to American Indians, adver-
tisements, and a poetry column.

In his first issue Whittier printed a poem by his sister,
signed E. H. W. Amesbury, in which she addressed the New
Hampshire delegation in Congress who voted for the Gag Rule as
"false servants of a people's trust." The next issue carried a poem
lamenting the death of a young minister, prefaced with the note:
"The following beautiful lines are from the pen of Lucy Hooper of
Brooklyn, N.Y. a young lady who has written some of the sweetest and purest poetry which has ever been published in this country." All his life Whittier was to be enthusiastic about the writings
of his friends, as if his affection blinded his critical eye.

In the same issue he followed Lucy's poem with his own "Farewell of a Virginia Slave Mother to her Daughters Sold into Southern Bondage."

Gone, gone;—sold and gone
To the rice-swamp dank and lone,
Where the slave-whip ceaseless swings,
Where the noisome insect stings,
Where the fever demon strews
Poison with the falling dews,
Where the sickly sunbeams glare
Through the hot and misty air;
Gone, gone—sold and gone
To the rice-swamp dank and lone.

There were five more similarly stirring stanzas. The piece was widely reprinted, and it increased Whittier's reputation as the poet of abolition.

Pennsylvania Hall was finished and in use even before the sidewalk in front of it was paved and curbed. One of the committee rooms on the first floor was occupied by the Pennsylvania Anti-Slavery Society, another by Benjamin Jones's bookstore, and a third by the office of the *Pennsylvania Freeman*. On the second floor was the great auditorium seating three thousand people and on the third, one seating eighteen hundred. It was modern and elegant in every way, from the fine mahogany furniture on the platform of the auditorium to the up-to-date gas lighting fixtures. Many places still depended on oil lamps and candles. The cost, which had been estimated at twenty thousand dollars, came in the end, not surprisingly, to more than fifty-seven thousand dollars. The *United States Gazette* called the big auditorium "the most spacious and elegant room of the kind in Philadelphia."

Opening ceremonies were planned for three days, May 14 to May 16. Whittier was writing an ode for the occasion.

7. Pennsylvania Hall

The dedication ceremonies opened at ten o'clock on the morning of May 14, 1838, with Daniel Neall, the chairman of the board, presiding. It was a great moment, the culmination of months of planning and of work. The beautiful hall, with its motto, "Virtue, Liberty, Independence," inscribed on the front of it, was filled. Black people were scattered over the big room, not confined to back seats. Notables in the antislavery movement sat upon the platform. Whittier with his notebook was taking down everything for the *Pennsylvania Freeman*.

Daniel Neall set forth briefly the purpose of the building, read letters from well-known persons who could not be there, and introduced the main speaker, David Paul Brown. A forty-five-year-old Philadelphia lawyer and playwright who had helped many a fugitive slave to get away safely, he proved to be a sad disappointment on this occasion. He announced that he favored *certain* abolition of slavery rather than *immediate* abolition. The slaves were not, he said, "morally or intellectually in a condition qualifying them for so sudden and important a change." He called for education of the slaves and the freeing of children born to them. It was, as Garrison said scornfully, "the old siren song of gradualism." His words sound strangely like what was still being said more than a century later during the struggle for integration of the schools.

In the afternoon the Philadelphia Lyceum had a meeting in the hall, and in the evening there was a lecture on temperance, during which a pane of glass was broken by a stone thrown from the street outside.

The second dedication session took place the next morning, when Whittier's ode was the first thing on the program. His shyness kept him off the platform, and Charles C. Burleigh, a young abolitionist from New England, read it for him. It was a stately poem with many classical allusions; it compared the Pantheon, the Parthenon, the Colosseum and other ancient structures built with slave labor to this fair new hall built by Christian free men to provide

A free arena for the strife of mind
To caste or sect or color unconfined.

The ode was followed by speeches on the wrongs done to the Cherokee and Seminole Indians. As is the case today the movement for justice to the Negro reminded Americans of the appalling wrongs they had done and were doing to the real owners of the land on which they lived. There was a discussion of the colonization scheme. William Lloyd Garrison, who was seen sitting in the gallery, was called to the platform, though he asked to be excused on the grounds of ill health. He then pointed out that so far no colored brother had been asked to take part in the ceremonies and said that Mr. Brown's speech the day before had "contained enough poison to kill all the colored men on earth."

During the day placards were posted on trees and awning poles over the city. "Whereas," they proclaimed, "a convention for the avowed purpose of effecting the immediate abolition of slavery in this Union is now in session in this city, it behooves all citizens who entertain a proper respect for the right of property and the preservation of the Constitution of the United States to interfere *forcibly* if they *must.*" It called on all who opposed abolition to assemble at the Pennsylvania Hall in Sixth Street the following morning at eleven o'clock and demand the end of the convention.

In spite of these threats, the audience that gathered inside the hall at ten the next morning was larger than ever. Outside in the street fifty or sixty people prowled about the doors, looked at the gas pipes, and made vague threats. The afternoon session adopted a resolution condemning the expulsion of the Cherokees from their land in Georgia. This closed the dedication program, but other meetings were scheduled for that night and all the next day.

In the evening a women's meeting, at which Lucretia Mott and others spoke, was interrupted by the smashing of windows and by hoots and yells from outside. When the meeting ended, white women went out arm in arm with their Black friends to protect them. Meanwhile two of the managers of the hall had gone to the police office to ask for protection and were told that the four men who had already been sent were all that were available. Those men had been given orders not to arrest anyone.

On the morning of May 17, when the Anti-Slavery Convention of American Women was meeting, an angry crowd began to assemble. A committee of the Board of Managers went to the mayor, who said, "There are two sides to every question. It is public opinion that makes mobs and 99 out of 100 of those with whom I converse are against you." Certain now that their hall was doomed, the committee, deeply troubled, left and called a meeting of the entire board. The crowd around the hall continued to grow larger.

At sunset the mayor said that he would disperse the mob if he were given the keys to the building. The evening meeting was called off and the mayor came to address the crowd. What he said was practically an invitation to violence. After expressing the mild hope that nothing of a disorderly nature would occur, he said, "We never call out the military here. We do not need such measures. Indeed I would, fellow citizens, look upon you as my police. . . . I now bid you farewell for the night."

The crowd gave three loud cheers for the mayor, and as soon as he was out of sight began to break windows and batter at doors with axes. It took about twenty minutes to bring a scantling, a big timber, and break down the front door with it. Sixth Street from Arch to Race streets was jammed with onlookers, who did nothing to oppose the rioters.

They poured through the broken doors, stormed into the Anti-Slavery Office and tossed books and papers out of the windows, went down to the cellar where they found wood shavings left by the builders, carried them upstairs, and piled them on the platform in the big auditorium. They tore down the newly painted Venetian blinds and added them to the pile, wrenched out the gas pipes and set fire to the whole. Flames lit up the windows and then the street and then the sky.

Outside in the street people came running to add to the confusion. The fire engines, when they got there, played their hoses on adjoining buildings to save them, but not a drop went on the burning hall. In the flames whipped by the fresh spring breeze the words "Virtue, Liberty, Independence" stood out ironically. From Sixth and Chestnut streets three blocks away the cracked Liberty Bell rang.

Whittier was there in the middle of the crowd, in anguish for the hall and for his papers. Some people shouted his name. Running into the house of Dr. Joseph Parrish, a well-known Quaker doctor and a member of the Underground Railroad, he borrowed a white overcoat and a wig. Thus disguised, he ran into the burning building to his office and gathered up what he could. He was especially concerned for the next issue of the *Freeman,* and in

POSTSCRIPT!
Atrocious outrage! Burning of Pennsylvania Hall!

18th of Fifth mo., half past 7 o'clock.—Pennsylvania Hall is in ashes! The beautiful temple consecrated to Liberty, has been offered a smoking sacrifice to the Demon of Slavery. In the heart of this city a flame has gone up to Heaven. It will be seen from Maine to Georgia. In its red and lurid light, men will see more clearly than ever the black abominations of the fiend at whose instigation it was kindled.

We have only time to give a hasty sketch of the horrible proceedings of last night. All day yesterday a body of ill-disposed persons lingered around the Hall. The crowd increased towards evening. Between 6 and 7 o'clock, the mayor *for the first time* made his appearance, and met the managers of the Hall. He told them that he could not protect the building unless the keys of it were placed in his hands—and earnestly requested them to put the Hall under his control for the evening. This was acquiesced in. He then addressed the crowd, who answered him with cheers, but refused to disperse. About 8 o'clock the work of destruction commenced in the midst of assembled thousands. The doors were broken open with axes,—the Anti-Slavery Office in the lower story was entered and the books and pamphlets scattered among the crowd. Soon the cry of fire was heard, and flames appeared from the building.

It was set on fire in several places: and the engines of the firemen were not permitted to play upon the Hall. Piles of shavings from the cellar were brought up to the speakers' forum, placed upon it, and set on fire. The flames soon rose high above the roof, casting a baleful light upon the busy incendiaries—and the immense crowd of human beings who filled all the adjoining streets. From 15,000 to 20,000 persons stood gazing on the scene.

We have no time for comment. Let the abhorrent deed speak for itself. Let all men see by what a frail tenure they hold property and life in a land overshadowed by the curse of Slavery.

his haste he did not manage to save Benjamin Lundy's papers. He was out again before the roof fell in.

When the roof went with a great crash and flames shot up into the sky, the mob yelled with delight, and one man was heard to shout, above the roaring and crackling of the fire, "Hurrah! That's liberty!"

Meanwhile at Lucretia Mott's house not far away on North Ninth Street, a group of friends, including J. Miller McKim and Charles Burleigh, were sitting in the parlor waiting for news, hearing the voices of the rioters pouring through Race Street and wondering if their turn would come next. About eleven o'clock Thomas Mott, Lucretia's son, burst in, shouting, "They're coming!" Lucretia Mott said next day, "It was a searching time. . . . I felt at the moment that I was willing to suffer whatever the cause required." But when the mob reached their corner, a friend shouted, "On to the Motts!" and led them off in the wrong direction.

William Lloyd Garrison, who was also in danger, was whisked out of town by a little band of friends headed by Robert Purvis, a Black man.

Whittier all this time was at work on the *Pennsylvania Freeman,* which was due to appear next day. He had rescued his pasted-up pages with the reports of the opening sessions; now he took out one of the prepared articles on the third page and substituted a hasty account of the fire. Fortunately only the editorial office was in the hall; the printing establishment on Arch Street was undisturbed. The paper went to press at seven thirty on the morning of the eighteenth and was out that afternoon with the unusal emphasis of a headline.

POSTSCRIPT! ATROCIOUS OUTRAGE!

Pennsylvania Hall is in ashes. The beautiful temple consecrated to Liberty has been offered a smoking sacrifice to the Demon of Slavery.

There followed a report of the steps taken to protect it, the mayor's negligence, and the final destruction.

The article ended:

> We have no time for comment. Let the abhorrent deed speak for itself. Let all men see by what frail tenure they hold property and life in a land overshadowed by slavery.

In an extra published later in the week, Whittier gave a full account of the events of May 16 and 17, step by step. To the charge that the sitting together of Blacks and whites in the meetings was unnecessarily provocative and aroused fury, he replied firmly, "We should have been false to our principles if we had refused to admit men of every sect, range and color, on terms of equality, to witness our proceedings."

On the morning after the fire, while small boys climbed over the smoking ruins in search of souvenirs, gangs attacked and burned a four-story brick orphanage for "colored" children, newly built by members of the Society of Friends. Fortunately the children had not yet been moved in. Rioters damaged Bethel Church at Sixth Street near Lombard, which was a Negro church, and surrounded the *Public Ledger* building, angry at the newspaper's criticism of mobism. The mayor provided protection for this building, and the attack was unsuccessful.

Later in the month Whittier attended the New England Anti-Slavery Convention in Boston. When a mob gathered around the Marlboro Chapel, where it was being held, and threatened to destroy it, the mayor of Boston, unlike the mayor of Philadelphia, took prompt action and the building was spared.

After spending a restful time at Joseph Healy's country place, Spring Grove Farm in Bucks County, Whittier settled in for the long hot Philadelphia summer.

It was not by any means a lonely time for him, for he had a

lively circle of young friends. Besides his cousins Ann and Margaret Wendell, there were three other Quaker girls, all named Elizabeth, who made much of him, collected his poems and called him, among themselves, the Bard.

Elizabeth Neall, the daughter of Daniel Neall, who had been chairman of the board of Pennsylvania Hall, lived on Arch Street. Sarah Lewis, the schoolteacher at the Healys', tried to promote an engagement between Elizabeth and Whittier but there was never anything more than a comfortable friendship between them. She married Sidney Howard Gay, and Whittier was still writing amusing letters to her when he was eighty.

Elisabeth Nicholson, three years younger than Whittier, was the daughter of Lindzey Nicholson, an influential Friend active in the Underground Railroad. She was a lively girl with a quick tongue. At this time she was keeping house for her twice-widowed father and bringing up two younger half-brothers. With her beautiful, spidery handwriting she was copying into two blank books all of Whittier's poems that she could get hold of: the verses he sent as excuses for not attending parties, those he wrote in autograph albums, and the like. She wrote poetry herself, which she showed to Whittier. When he ventured to suggest some improvements, she flared up indignantly. He hastened to apologize; his improvements, he admitted, like Sheridan's Irishman, improved the poem in the wrong way. Possibly feeling that he was not serious enough, she remained huffy. "She has not forgiven me," he wrote to Elizabeth Lloyd, "and I am not quite sure that she ought to."

The third Elizabeth, a year younger than Elisabeth Nicholson, was the beautiful, poetic, and sensitive daughter of Isaac Lloyd, a well-to-do merchant and a strict orthodox Friend, who disapproved of the abolition movement and Whittier too. Whittier had committed the further crime of quoting Shakespeare, and Shakespeare was forbidden to the ten Lloyd children. They lived in a house on Union Street near St. Peter's Church, and they were very hospitable to the right kind of Friends. At Yearly Meeting time the house was filled with visiting Quakers and Elizabeth was put out of her room. "I am glad to see the Friends come," she said, "but *delighted* to see them go." She too wrote poetry—her poem "Milton's Prayer of Patience" was especially admired—and she made the illustrations for Elisabeth Nicholson's albums of Whittier's poems: delicate, softly tinted, tiny landscapes.

There were expeditions out of the city to the Wissahickon Creek, on the bank of which there was an inn that served catfish and waffles, and to the famous waterworks at Fairmount on the Schuylkill. "It is a beautiful place," Greenleaf wrote to his sister. "Nature has done much but art infinitely more; fountains are made to gush up from the rocks of the cliffs which overhang the Schuylkill through the mouths of images carved out of marble. . . . I have been out in the country frequently. Send me the two 'poetries' as soon as possible."

The 'poetries' were two of his poems, "The Fratricide" and "The Pharisee," which he wanted for a volume that Joseph Healy was proposing to publish in the fall. It was to contain 180 pages, with fifty poems, half of which were to be antislavery poems and half of a more general nature. Whittier selected the poems himself, and he dedicated the volume to his friend, Henry Stanton. On the title page he quoted a passage from the English poet, Samuel Taylor Coleridge, which ended with the words, "Truth should be spoken at all times but more especially at those times when to speak truth is dangerous."

Before the book was out, Whittier, ill and miserable, had gone back to Amesbury to be cared for by his mother and sister. He edited the *Freeman* by mail until his return to Philadelphia in the following April.

One enthusiastic admirer got a copy of the volume from Benjamin Jones's bookstore in Arch Street and read it all the way home as she walked along the street. When she came near her own

Landscape by Elizabeth Lloyd for Elisabeth Nicholson's album

door she saw company approaching, who she knew would stay all day. Walking very slowly and holding her umbrella in front of her face until they were safely in the house, she scurried through the alleyway, in at the back door, and up to her own room, where she shut the door and bolted it. Then Elizabeth Lloyd settled down in the fireless, chilly room and read all fifty poems, one right after another.

8. A Turning Point

Whittier was back in Philadelphia for three months in the spring of 1839, but he was still suffering from head and chest pain. Early in July he persuaded his friend and second cousin, Moses Cartland, a teacher in Weare, New Hampshire, to take over the editorship of the *Freeman* for the summer months while he himself went off with Henry Stanton on a trip into the Pennsylvania Dutch country. The American Anti-Slavery Society hoped to enlist seventy speakers to go about and lecture on abolition, and Whittier and Stanton were to try to find some of them in Pennsylvania theological schools.

Henry Brewster Stanton, two years older than Whittier, was descended from a line of distinguished Puritans of New England. He was handsome and charming and perhaps the most eloquent of the abolitionist speakers: quick-witted, compassionate, strong, with a sense of humor that captivated his audiences. It was Stanton who made the public addresses on the trip that he and Whittier took together.

They got up too late on the morning of July 7 to have breakfast as they had planned with the Nicholsons on Arch Street.

Instead, as Whittier wrote to Elizabeth, they had execrable tea, ham tough and solid as sheet iron, and greasy hot cakes at a "dirty Dutch tavern" where the train stopped after two hours. There was a second stop for lunch before they reached Harrisburg and "a splendid hotel" at three o'clock. From Harrisburg they went on to Carlisle, where they stayed with Miller McKim, now pastor of a church at nearby Womelsdorf. The next day they visited Governor Ritner, who had retired to the country after having been defeated in the last election by proslavery interests.

"The old man was out on his farm and his wife and daughters welcomed us with great hospitality. The governor soon came in in his working dress." After the destruction of Pennsylvania Hall Ritner had immediately offered a reward of $500 for the apprehension of the instigators of the outrage, which shamed the mayor of Philadelphia into doing the same thing, though grudgingly and belatedly. Nothing came of either offer, and not much from the investigations of the insurance commission. Though there were great hopes for rebuilding the hall, they could never get enough money, and in the end the lot was sold to the Order of Odd Fellows.

From Carlisle Whittier and Stanton went to Chambersburg and then to Gettysburg, where they tried to rouse the ministerial students at the Lutheran Seminary to go out and speak for the cause. They got one speaker, but for the most part Whittier found the Pennsylvania Dutch apathetic on the subject of slavery: "thrice dead and plucked up by the roots." Henry Stanton remembered afterward that Whittier cheered him "with his genial presence and wise counsel." Whittier had a bubbling sense of humor, often expressed with a straight face, which deceived people into thinking him serious, sometimes to his embarrassment. After the Pennsylvania trip he and Stanton went to the annual meeting of the American Anti-Slavery Society in Albany.

At this meeting a division in the society that had been quietly growing for some time broke out into the open. The issue was political action. Whittier, Stanton, the Tappan brothers, James G. Birney, and others believed that slavery could be brought to an end by electing men pledged to vote against it. Garrison and his group on the other hand had lost faith in the U.S. Constitution and in political action through it. They wished, moreover, to work for other reforms besides abolition, for peace, women's rights, and temperance. Whittier, though he wholeheartedly favored these causes, believed that slavery was the chief enemy and that all their efforts should be concentrated on doing away with it. A committee, of which Whittier and Stanton were members, proposed that the abolitionists nominate candidates for president and vice-president in the election of 1840. Garrison protested, but the resolution was passed. This was the beginning of the Liberty Party, which nominated James G. Birney for president in the following year and again in 1844.

It was also the end, for a time, of the close friendship between Garrison and Whittier—to Whittier's great regret. Garrison became very critical of Whittier and made harsh remarks about him, which Whittier overlooked in his effort to keep their relationship as it used to be. When those who believed in political action formed a new organization called the American and Foreign Anti-Slavery Society, Whittier declined to serve on its board. As time went on he paid less attention to antislavery meetings and more to political action itself.

From the meeting in Albany Whittier went to the fashionable Saratoga Springs to rest and drink the water. He found it "rascally," but he enjoyed very much the "travel, exercise and open air" and the gaiety of the place. He found "ten thousand ridiculous things" to amuse him and longed to have somebody to laugh with about them. "As it is I have laughed alone," he wrote to a Philadelphia friend, "and that is hard business."

Before the Civil War many rich Southerners came from their plantations to spend the summer in the white-pillared, red-carpeted, palm-decorated hotels there. Whittier made friends with a man from Mississippi and two from South Carolina. He got along well with Southerners, even though he eagerly seized the opportunity to lay, as he said, his principles before their minds. Like John Woolman a century earlier he never considered the slave-holder himself the enemy, only the institution of slavery. He urged on all abolitionists the principle of treating "our Southern friends as intelligent and high-minded men," who were not responsible for the introduction of slavery into the country; they had inherited it, not created it.

After Saratoga he went as usual to Newport to the Yearly Meeting and so home to Amesbury.

While he was there Lucy Hooper was visiting in Newburyport and hoping daily that he would come to see her. She wrote to her sister Harriet in August, "Not a glimpse, not a line have I had, so that in consequence I am quite congealed and have only to solace myself by repeating the old song,

> *There's nobody coming for thee, my dear Jane,*
> *I've looked out at the gate and up at the lane,*
> *There's nobody coming for thee!*

To what to attribute this I am entirely at a loss."

But just as she was writing this letter, Whittier drove up. She broke another engagement in order to take a drive with him. They went up to the bridge and looked at the Merrimack, and the next day she went to the village called The Rocks with him. But when he was in New York the following year, he did not find time to call on her.

He included one of her poems in a little book called *The North Star,* which he edited that winter to be sold at an antislavery fair. Other poems in it were written by John Quincy Adams; James T. Fields, a young editor in Boston; Elizabeth Lloyd; and Elizabeth Whittier. His own poems in it were "The Exiles" and "The World's Convention."

He went back to Philadelphia in October and took his sister Elizabeth with him. It was probably during this winter that he had his picture painted by the well-known Philadelphia portraitist, Bass Otis. Isaac Wendell wanted it and engaged Otis for the work. Even though it was not easy to pin the busy Whittier down for sittings, the portrait was a success. It caught the ardent, dark-eyed poet in a moment of alert attention.

Ann Wendell, who was an invalid and spent much of her time on the sofa in the family living room, told how the artist got the expression he wanted. "Otis placed him at a table, turned his attention to something else and then addressed him a little suddenly with, 'Mr. Whittier!' When Greenleaf started up to respond, he said, 'Keep that position' and he was so taken."

Though he enjoyed his friends there and liked what he called "the Quaker purity of this city and its Quaker hospitality," he grew tired of brick walls, and he never felt well there. In February he resigned from the *Freeman* altogether, and Charles C. Burleigh succeeded him as editor.

On his resignation the directors of the Anti-Slavery Society of Pennsylvania passed a resolution praising both his discharge of his duties as editor and his character "in the private walks of social life." As a token of their admiration they appointed him their representative to the World Convention of antislavery societies to be held in London in the summer of 1840.

He and Elizabeth returned to Amesbury, taking a week to get there. With him he took two souvenirs of Philadelphia that he kept all his life. One was a facsimile of the Declaration of Sentiments of 1833 framed in wood from Pennsylvania Hall and the other a walnut cane also made from Pennsylvania Hall wood. He never used any other walking stick, and one of his most effective abolitionist poems, "The Relic," was about this cane.

Portrait by Bass Otis

He expected to go to the convention in London and looked forward eagerly to the sea voyage as well as to visiting England and meeting English Friends. But as the time drew near his friend and physician, Dr. Henry L. Bowditch, advised strongly against it, and he reluctantly gave up the plan.

The convention is remembered now for having refused to admit Lucretia Mott and Elizabeth Stanton solely because they were women. Elizabeth Stanton was the attractive and lively bride of Henry, who was himself one of the delegates to the convention. She and Lucretia Mott, who met for the first time in London, became lifelong friends and sister workers for women's suffrage. Several years after their experience in London they organized a history-making convention of American women.

Whittier did, however, attend the Yearly Meeting in Newport, which turned out to be one of the high experiences of his life. He had been to Yearly Meeting many times before and enjoyed seeing his friends there, but this time was different and in its way as crucial in his life as the writing of *Justice and Expediency*.

He went there under a good deal of inner stress, not feeling well enough to attend every session. "It seems strange sometimes that I cannot do as others around me," he wrote to Elizabeth. He was now thirty-two. He had poor health with no prospect of improvement. He had no job. Most of his poems were dashed off at top speed to influence people against slavery—turning the crank of an opinion mill, he was to call it. He received no money for them. Because of his well-known stand on abolition, literary magazines like *Harper's* would not publish his poems on other subjects. He liked women but he could not afford to marry, for he had to support his mother, his aunt, and his sister.

At Newport, the beautiful old town on Narraganset Bay, more than three thousand Friends gathered to sit in a deep silence together, waiting for the inward stirrings of the Spirit, to transact the business of the Society, to exchange news, to avoid, so far as possible, taking a stand on the immediate abolition of slavery and, this year, to listen in awe and admiration to the eloquent English Quaker, Joseph John Gurney, then on a long visit to America. Gurney, the brother of the great prison reformer Elizabeth Fry, was so popular among Friends and was so widely and lavishly entertained that for a century afterward Quaker housewives called the leftovers after a party Joseph-Johns. He spoke to the Friends in Newport in 1840 about the heroic and inspiring life of the English Quaker Daniel Wheeler, who had recently died. Whittier was deeply moved by this talk.

Something profound happened to Whittier during this time in Newport. Always reserved about his own inner life, he did not tell just what it was, but he gave Ann Wendell a glimpse in a letter. After they had attended a meeting with Gurney on abolition matters, Whittier and Richard Mott, an older Friend from the Purchase, New York, Meeting, took a long walk together. "During our walk," Whittier wrote to Ann,

> he told me he knew not how it was or why but that his mind had been drawn into a deep and extraordinary exercise of sympathy with me; that he had been sensible of a deep trial and exercise in my own mind; that he felt it so strongly that he could not rest easy without informing me of it, although he had heard nothing and seen nothing to produce this conviction in his mind. He felt desirous to offer me the language of encouragement, to urge me to put aside every weight that encumbers and to look unto Him who was able to deliver me from every trial. I confess I was startled. . . . I said little to him but enough to show him something of the state of my mind. Pray for me that I may not suffer this most evident day of the Lord's visitation to pass over and leave me as before.

Whatever the "visitation" that had come to his troubled spirit, it had been recognized by an older and respected Friend, who had taken him away from the crowd in order to give him encouragement. This very recognition, authenticating his subjective experience, must have impressed its reality upon him. He saw that it must change his life.

After this experience his humor bubbled up as spontaneously as ever; he was as ardent an abolitionist, as astute a political strategist; but he had a new calm and depth, a serene faith as well as unwavering determination. He read widely in mystical literature, searching for the meaning of life, for the experience and beliefs common to all religions. He began to write poems in which his gropings and discoveries were expressed. A poem published in 1848 called "The Wish of Today" shows how far he had come from his early ambitions.

> *I ask not now for gold to gild*
> *With mocking shine a weary frame;*
> *The yearning of the mind is stilled,*
> *I ask not now for Fame.*
>
> . . .
>
> *But, bowed in lowliness of mind,*
> *I make my humble wishes known;*
> *I only ask a will resigned,*
> *Oh, Father, to Thine own!*
>
> . . .
>
> *Though oft, like letters traced on sand*
> *My weak resolves have passed away,*
> *In mercy lend Thy helping hand*
> *Unto my prayer today!*

9. An English Friend

After the heights of his experiences at Newport, the inspiration of Joseph John Gurney, the sensitive understanding of Richard Mott, Whittier went back to Amesbury, to the little town with its dusty summer roads and the little meeting house where only a few Friends gathered together. If a word was spoken out of the silence, it was probably spoken by someone who said the same thing each week and said it badly in a singsong voice.

Whittier wrote rather sadly to Richard Mott of "sitting down in our small meeting and feeling in myself and in the meeting generally a want of life." It frequently happens in the religious life that a high experience is followed by a painful letdown, as if to test the steadfastness of the person who has been privileged to have his moments of insight and exaltation.

The winter was a quiet, rather dreary, one, when he felt so ill that he could not write or read for more than half an hour at a time, and even a visit to his friends in Haverhill fourteen miles away seemed too much for him. But early in April, with the coming of the spring, came an exciting visitor from England, and the young man for whom the drive to Haverhill had been too much rose up with determination and set out with the English Friend for Philadelphia and Baltimore.

Joseph Sturge was a well-to-do businessman from Birmingham, a generous philanthropist and a gentle reformer. He had been active in persuading the English Parliament to emancipate the slaves in the British colonies, and now he was eager to see what could be done in the United States. Unlike George Thompson, whose unsuccessful trip he had helped to finance, he planned to make no public addresses. He intended chiefly to visit Friends and to urge them to work more actively for abolition. He had heard about Whittier, probably from George Thompson, but had never met him. In February he wrote to Whittier explaining the purpose of his trip and asking him to travel with him and introduce him to Friends.

After a miserable three-and-a-half-weeks' crossing of the Atlantic through dangerous storms, in which an American ship was lost, Sturge arrived in New York on April 4. Whittier was there to meet him, and they liked each other at once. Sturge wrote to his sister that he found Whittier "all I could ask for a companion." Whittier for his part saw a short, stocky, ruddy-faced man of forty-eight with bushy eyebrows over gray eyes and a face that lit up with an expression of great sweetness and kindness. "I never met a gentler man," Whittier said later, "nor a firmer one."

Except for two periods when Whittier became exhausted and had to go home to rest, he spent the next four months traveling with his new friend. After a few days in New York, where Sturge met the Tappan brothers, they went on to Philadelphia and attended the Yearly Meeting there. They visited Baltimore, where they saw a slave-trading establishment, and attended a Baptist triennial convention, which voted dismally to exclude abolitionists from its board of foreign missions. They went next to Wilmington in Delaware, which was a slave state. Sturge went up the Hudson alone by boat and visited Albany, and then he and Whittier went

Joseph Sturge

together to New England Yearly Meeting in Newport. There the old and conservative Quakers who dominated the meeting refused to allow Joseph Sturge to speak in the meeting house on the emancipation of slaves in the West Indies. Whittier was grieved, embarrassed, and angered, and in protest he did not go to Yearly Meeting in Newport for several years after that.

They returned to Philadelphia and after a few days went on to Washington. There they listened to a heated debate in Congress on the Gag Rule that threatened to cut off petitions against slavery. They met and talked with President Tyler, John Quincy Adams, and Henry Clay. Clay asked Whittier why he had deserted him after being his warm friend earlier, and Whittier replied that he could not support a man who not only kept slaves himself but approved the extension of slavery to new states. Of the three, seventy-four-year-old John Quincy Adams, the fiery and indomitable ex-president who did his greatest work as a member of the House of Representatives, was the one whom Whittier loved and admired. Throughout his years in Congress John Quincy Adams stoutly defended the right of petition even when he did not approve of the petitions themselves.

In Washington too they visited the notorious slave pen where slaves were kept before being auctioned and the wretched jail which had caused the death of Reuben Crandall. Much later Whittier recalled it in a poem:

> *Beside me gloomed the prison cell*
> *Where wasted one in slow decline*
> *For uttering simple words of mine*
> *And loving freedom all too well.*

They talked with legislators, Quakers, and church members, trying, as Whittier said, "to fan into life the all but expiring embers of abolition." It was discouraging to him to find even Quakers so lukewarm. "It was not on my own account," he wrote to a cousin, "that I felt uneasiness—I am used to such things—but I felt keenly for my English friend."

To Elizabeth's great pleasure they had a few days in the Whittier home in Amesbury. "How we loved Joseph Sturge!" she wrote. And they visited many New England towns and Meetings. At length at the end of August Whittier saw his friend off on the *Caledonia* from Boston. Before he left, Sturge gave a thousand dollars to Whittier to be used for travel, personal expenses, or for antislavery work as he thought best. Whittier used it to support a new newspaper that the American and Foreign Abolition Society was trying to get started in New York.

The two, Whittier and Sturge, never saw each other again, though Sturge more than once offered to pay for a trip to England if Whittier and Elizabeth would go, but the friendship continued to flourish through letters as long as Sturge lived.

At home in Amesbury in August Whittier read in a Boston newspaper of the death of Lucy Hooper at twenty-five. He wrote at once to her sister, expressing his sympathy and sorrow and the shock that he felt. In her reply she hinted that Lucy had been heartbroken and her health had suffered as a result of her love for him and his lack of response. He wrote back at once a long letter, in which he said:

> My feelings toward her were those of a brother. I admired and loved her; yet felt myself compelled to crush every warmer feeling—poverty, protracted illness and our separate faiths—the pledge that I had made of all the hopes and dreams of my younger years to the cause of Freedom— compelled me to steel myself against everything which tended to attract me—the blessing of a woman's love and a home.

He was greatly troubled, regretting what appeared to be his "coldness," and he hated the thought that he might have wounded

Lucy's feelings. It seems likely, however, that Lucy's sister in her grief had read more into Lucy's feelings about Whittier than was actually there. They had had a literary and somewhat sentimental friendship, and if Whittier had allowed Lucy to hope for more, he was unconscious of the fact.

A little volume of Lucy's poems was published the next years under the title, *Poetical Remains of Lucy Hooper*. In some of them she complained of a lover's indifference. Whittier contributed a preface and a poem beginning, "They tell me, Lucy, thou art dead" and referring nostalgically to their walk along the Merrimack two years earlier.

Lays of My Home and Other Verse, Whittier's second volume of poems, was published in 1843, by the young editor who had contributed a poem to the *North Star*, James T. Fields, now a partner in the firm of Ticknor and Fields of Boston. It contained twenty-four poems, some of them ballads made from the tales Whittier had heard as a child, such as "The Old Wife and the New," some of them expressions of his philosophy, such as "Ego." In "Ego" he stated very clearly a fact that many of even the most ardent abolitionists did not understand: it was not only freedom that the Negro needed and was entitled to but respect as a human being as well. In the North, where Blacks were free, they suffered—and after all these years still do—from an often unconscious condescension and disrespect that undercuts their self-confidence and even their humanity.

Upon my ear not all in vain
Came the sad captive's clanking chain,
The groaning from his bed of pain.

And sadder still I saw the woe
Which only wounded spirits know
When Pride's strong footsteps o'er them go.

Spurned not alone in walks abroad
But from the temples of the Lord
Thrust out, apart like things abhorred. . . .

Oppressed and spoiled on every side,
By Prejudice and Scorn and Pride,
Life's common courtesies denied.

"The Christian Slave" resulted from an account he had
read of a slave auction in New Orleans, in which the auctioneer
described one female slave as "a good Christian." The poem,
which was written with angry sarcasm, had some unforgettable
lines:

A Christian! Going, gone!
Who bids for God's own image?

A poem called "Memories" went back to his Academy
days in Haverhill and told of the "beautiful and happy girl," Mary
Emerson Smith, and their walks along the Merrimack.

Ah! memories of sweet summer eves,
Of moonlit waves and willowy way,
Of stars and flowers and dewy leaves,
And smiles and tones more dear than they!

He wrote about New England and his love of nature; he included some of his new meditations on religion. In "To ———
with a copy of Woolman's *Journal*" he affirmed his faith in the
inward vision, which must be carried out in action:

Only in the gathered silence
Of a calm and waiting frame,
Light and wisdom as from Heaven
To the seeker came.

Not to idle dreams and trances,
  Length of face and solemn tone
But to Faith in <u>daily</u> striving
  And performance shown. . . .

Earnest toil and strong endeavor
  Of a spirit which within
Wrestles with familiar evil
  And besetting sin;

And without, with tireless vigor,
  Steady heart and weapon strong,
In the power of truth assailing
  Every form of wrong.

Though he had a contract on this book which called for royalties, actually all he received were some free copies of the book itself. His financial situation was precarious.

The following year he got a job in Lowell for six months, editing a newspaper called the *Middlesex Standard*, an organ of the Liberty Party. Lowell, a fast-growing city at the confluence of the Merrimack and Concord rivers, had abundant waterpower for the new textile mills, which were changing the character of life in New England and threatening the beauty of its villages. From lonely farms in New Hampshire and Maine and Massachusetts girls were coming to work in the mills with a feeling of adventure and freedom. For the first time they made money of their own, among companions of their own age; many of them found partners and married. Some of them published a literary paper called the *Lowell Offering*, which attained a circulation of four thousand in its five-year existence.

Whittier looked upon this new way of life in Essex County, and he saw both good and bad in it. He saw that for the first time woman's labor was accepted on the same level as man's; this

Cotton mills at Lowell

meant freedom for her, and that was good. He saw also that the hours were cruelly long, that the work itself was monotonous, and the noise of the clacking looms was deadly.

Roaming the city with clear and open eyes, he wrote of what he saw in a series of essays that he called "The Stranger in Lowell." He saw, for instance, that both employer and employee wished to keep the profits high, and for that reason neither really wanted to reduce the long hours. "Work," he wrote, "is here the patron saint." He did not have the Puritan attitude toward work but the Quaker point of view of John Woolman, who thought that men should work only long enough to earn the necessities of life and after that devote their time to their families, to wholesome pursuits of leisure, and their religious duties.

"Labor graduated to man's simple wants, necessities and unperverted tastes," wrote Whittier, "is doubtless well; but all beyond this is weariness to flesh and spirit. Every web which falls from these restless looms has a history more or less connected with sin and suffering, beginning with slavery and ending with over-work and premature death."

Thinking back to the days of his youth, when work was done by man's hands and not by machines, he began to write a series of poems about the men whose kind of labor was beginning to disappear, the drovers who every spring drove the cattle up into the mountain pastures of Vermont and New Hampshire and in the autumn drove them back again; the fishermen, the cobblers, the sailors, the lumbermen, the shipbuilders, the huskers, who came to a farm at harvest time and husked the corn.

While he was in Lowell, he went to a meeting of a club called the Improvement Circle, where a young mill worker who had contributed several poems to the *Lowell Offering* read one of them, "Sabbath Bells." Her name was Lucy Larcom. She was twenty and she had been working in the mill ever since she was eleven, when her mother had brought her family to Lowell. Her father, who had been a shipmaster and then a storekeeper in Beverly, Massachusetts, had died, and her mother, to support herself and her children, opened a boardinghouse for girls who worked in the mills.

Whittier, interested in the bright, sweet, ambitious young girl and seeing promise in her poems, took her to Amesbury to meet his mother and sister, who welcomed her warmly. A year or two later Lucy's elder sister married a man from Alton, Illinois, and the whole family went to live there. Later Lucy was to return to Massachusetts and renew her friendship with the Whittier family.

Whittier's next two books were both prose: *The Stranger in Lowell*, a collection of the papers that had appeared in the *Middlesex Standard*, and a small volume of essays entitled *The Supernaturalism of New England*. This was a continuation of his interest in the legends of his countryside that he had tried, unsuccessfully, to express in his very first book. After this he left the gathering of folklore—the term was invented by an English writer in this same year—to other people, although many of his later poems told stories of phantom ships, witches, changelings, ghosts, and other supernatural phenomena.

10. The National Era

As early as 1842 Whittier had foreseen the annexation of Texas and its admission to the Union as a slave state. Angrily he had written to Samuel E. Sewall, "If Texas is to be added to us, as there are no doubtful indications, let us say, Disunion before Texas!" In the spring of 1844 he published a heated poem in the Boston *Courier*, "Texas: Voice of New England," in which he called on the South to

> *Take your slavery-blackened vales,*
> *Leave us but our own free gales,*
> *Blowing on our thousand sails.*

He opposed strongly in many editorials in the *Middlesex Standard* the re-election of James K. Polk, who was pledged to annexation. Polk, however, was elected and immediately moved to fulfill his pledge. In December 1845 the Liberty Party sent Whittier and another man to Washington with a petition to Congress, signed by 60,000 people, against the annexation of Texas. It was too late to have any effect—if indeed petitions ever did have much effect. Texas was admitted to the Union as a slave state on December 29, 1845.

Whittier's poem "At Washington" described the "half-built town" and the sharp contrasts between the glittering parlors of the rich and the horrors of the slave prison near the capitol. He ended the poem with a plea for unity in doing the work that must be done for freedom.

With the defeat of the Liberty Party candidate in Essex County in the elections of 1844, the *Middlesex Standard* came to an end. Whittier had already gone back to Amesbury, where he was a well-known figure. He liked to drop into the village grocery on his way to the post office, and, sitting on a cracker barrel, talk over the news of the day with the men who gathered there. This was his chance to air his views and contribute a fresh and perhaps unpopular opinion. He was without a job.

At one time Whittier considered the possibility of going West, as so many other New Englanders were doing. The New England farms were stony and hilly, and the soil was poor. There was a great deal of fertile land in the West to be had for little money and much work. Quakers had settled in Salem, Iowa, which had been admitted into the Union as the twenty-ninth state. Whittier thought he might go there to help start a Liberty Party. But a better opportunity opened up for him. The New York newspaper of the American and Foreign Anti-Slavery Society having failed, the Society decided to start a weekly paper in Washington to be called the *National Era*. This time, in order to attract readers, they would include literary and travel essays and poems, as well as abolitionist articles. They invited Whittier to be a corresponding editor. He could work at home and would receive modest fees for his contributions.

The editor in chief was a courageous man seasoned in the cause of abolition. Dr. Gamaliel Bailey had published in Cincinnati the first antislavery paper west of the Appalachians and had proved himself brave in the face of repeated mob attacks. The year after he came to Washington to edit the *National Era* an angry crowd gathered in front of the office and threatened to burn it down, but the mayor of Washington protected it. On the third day the mob arrived at Bailey's house. He came out on the front steps and talked reasonably to them, explaining his ideas and purposes. From then on he had no further trouble.

The first issue of the *National Era* appeared on January 1, 1847, with three contributions in it by Whittier. One was a poem, "Randolph of Roanoke," a tribute to the great Virginian who in his will had freed his slaves and provided funds to buy land for them in Ohio. Whittier had long admired Randolph, and his poem, written soon after Randolph's death fourteen years earlier, had been waiting for the right occasion to be published. The other two pieces were prose.

During the thirteen years that the *National Era* lasted, Whittier contributed over 100 poems to it and 275 pieces of prose. The nearest thing to a novel that Whittier ever wrote, *Stray Leaves from the Journal of Margaret Smith*, appeared first in the *Era* in serial form in 1848. It was published as a book the following year with the title *Margaret Smith's Journal*.

Margaret Smith, the heroine, a gay, warm-hearted young girl from England, was visiting her relatives in the Massachusetts colony in 1678–79 and recording her impressions of the new country in her diary. Not bound by the rigorous Puritan ideas of her hosts, she was sympathetic to the persecuted Quakers, though she did not understand them, and she was interested in the Indians whom she encountered. The story was a slight one about Margaret's cousin, Rebecca Rawson, who married a handsome but worthless visiting Englishman instead of the solid homespun friend of her childhood. But the picture of the country, its forests, its lakes and seasons, its farms, its sturdy colonists, its Indians, was authentic and interesting. No one else, before or since, has quite equaled Whittier's reconstruction of that period. Professor Edward Wagenknecht has called it "one of the inexplicably neglected classics of American literature."

A serialized novel followed Whittier's in the *Era*. It was to have an enormous influence on the thought and emotions of the American people. Harriet Beecher Stowe's *Uncle Tom's Cabin* was immediately popular, and it also assured the success of the *National Era*. Hawthorne's famous short story "The Great Stone Face" appeared in the *Era* on Whittier's recommendation, and there were many stories by a popular novelist, Mrs. E. D. E. N. Southworth. Whittier also wrote essays on seventeenth-century characters whom he admired, Andrew Marvell, John Milton, John Bunyan, and Thomas Ellwood, and on his contemporary friends, Bayard Taylor, Lydia Maria Child, and Oliver Wendell Holmes. These and others were reprinted in a volume called *Old Portraits and Modern Sketches*.

The great issues of the years leading up to the Civil War marched through the pages of the *National Era*, and Whittier had his comments in prose or verse on all of them.

What was called the Compromise of 1850 roused some of his strongest feelings. The compromise was actually not one but five statutes by which the North and the South each won something it wanted and gave up some principle held dear. Territorial governments were established in New Mexico and Utah, to be slave or free as the inhabitants should decide. The South allowed the slave trade in the District of Columbia to be abolished. The North yielded reluctantly to a new and stronger Fugitive Slave Law, which required that Negroes who had escaped to free states must be captured and returned to their masters, with severe penalties for those who failed to do so. These acts were debated long and brilliantly in Congress, and Daniel Webster, the great liberal orator of whom New England was so proud, eloquently urged their passage in the belief that they would save the Union.

Whittier was outraged to the very depth of his being by what he saw as Webster's cold-blooded desertion of the cause of the slave. He wrote in fury his most spare and bitter poem, "Ichabod." It was one of his best poems and also one of the best of its kind ever written—the polemic, or poem of denunciation. *Ichabod* is a Hebrew word meaning "the glory has departed." There were nine four-line stanzas, somber and relentless, beginning:

> *So fallen! So lost! the light withdrawn*
> > *Which once he wore!*
> *The glory from his gray hairs gone*
> > *Forevermore!*
>
> *Revile him not, the tempter hath*
> > *A snare for all;*
> *And pitying tears, not scorn and wrath*
> > *Befit his fall!*

It goes on to say: he who might have led has fallen back; let us not insult him now but instead utter a lament, as if he had died; nothing is left of all that we loved in him but power. The poem ends:

> *All else is gone; from those great eyes*
> > *The soul has fled:*
> *When faith is lost, when honor dies,*
> > *The man is dead!*
>
> *Then pay the reverence of old days*
> > *To his dead fame;*
> *Walk backward with averted gaze,*
> > *And hide the shame!*

The poem appeared in the *National Era* for May 2, 1850, and afterward in Whittier's book, *Songs of Labor and Other Poems*, published by James T. Fields that summer.

Thirty years later, when he was seventy-two, Whittier wrote another poem on Daniel Webster, which he called "The Lost Occasion." In it he spoke of Webster as "New England's stateliest type of man" and said he should have lived to see the Civil War.

> *No stronger voice than thine had then*
> *Called out the utmost might of men,*
> *To make the Union's charter free*
> *And strengthen law by liberty.*

It was not nearly so fine a poem as "Ichabod," but he directed that in every edition of his poems it should stand next to "Ichabod" as a sort of apology for its harshness.

Whittier's stand on the abolition of slavery, in those years when he labored to influence public opinion, was still not the most extreme one. He believed that it could be accomplished without the horror of war and violence and without the dissolution of the Union. Untiringly he insisted that no territory and no new state admitted to the Union should be allowed to hold slaves. He did not demand that Congress interfere with slavery in the states where it had been long established; he thought that, confined and isolated in those states, it would inevitably die.

Not all the poems that he published in the *National Era* were antislavery poems. He wrote, for instance, a tribute to the Russian poet, Alexander Pushkin, who was proud of his great-grandfather, an Ethiopian slave. Some of Whittier's *Songs of Labor* had come out first in the *National Era* as well as some of his poems about New England and the beauty of its countryside. "The Last Walk in Autumn" vividly describes the New England fall, his contentment with his home and the friends who came to see him there, his faith in the future.

I have not seen, I may not see,
  My hopes for man take form in fact,
But God will give the victory
  In due time; in that faith I act.

One of the most famous of all his poems, "Maud Muller," was first published in the *National Era*. It was a tale in rhymed couplets of a rich judge who, riding along a dusty road in summer, saw a young girl working in the field and asked her for a cup of water from the roadside spring. She handed it to him, and the poem tells the thoughts of each as he drank from her tin cup. He saw the fresh and gentle young girl and imagined himself a harvester, relieved of the heavy burdens of his office, free to love her and to live a simple life. She for her part imagined herself the wife of such a man, graceful, rich, able to help those whom she loved. Each had an idealized picture of the other's life. Their ways parted but in after years both remembered the moment by the dusty road. The poem ends:

  Of all sad words of tongue or pen
  The saddest are these, It might have been!

It was immediately popular, quoted far and wide, recited by schoolchildren on Speech Days and, inevitably, parodied. One of the first and best parodies was by Whittier himself:

  Of all good words of pen or verse
  The best are these: It might be worse!

God pity them both & pity us all
Who vainly the dreams of life recall!

For of all sad words of tongue or pen
The saddest are these: "It might have been!"

Ah well! for us all some sweet hope lies
Deeply buried from human eyes,

And in the hereafter angels may
Roll the stone from its grave away!

John G. Whittier

11. Politics

Although he spent much of his time writing for the *National Era,* writing did not occupy the whole of Whittier's life during the years of that influential and absorbing paper. He was active in politics behind the scenes, going to political meetings (though seldom making speeches), talking to politicians, giving advice, mapping strategy for campaigns, and writing letters in his fine, neat handwriting. On election day he was always in Amesbury, seeing his fellow townsmen in the grocery store, the newsstand, the post office, the drugstore, expressing his opinions, which they respected for their sincerity and independence. In a poem called "The Eve of Election" he urged men to vote conscientiously.

> *The crowning fact,*
> *The kingliest act*
> *Of Freedom is the freeman's vote!*

His friend Charles Sumner was an important part of his political life. In 1829 when Whittier at twenty-one was editing the *American Manufacturer,* a tall (six feet four), handsome Harvard student of eighteen came into the office about a printing job for his father. It was a casual meeting not repeated for many years. Charles Sumner went on to study at the Harvard Law School, and after getting his degree, he spent a few months in Washington. His father could open many doors for him, and he wanted to observe the workings of the Supreme Court and the Congress. He returned to Boston disillusioned, unable to look upon politics "with anything but loathing," and went to the Harvard Law School to teach. After sixteen years Whittier encountered him again, and the second time it was over a Fourth of July oration.

Independence Day in those times was the big day of the year, celebrated in every town by a parade, the firing of an ancient cannon, an oration, a picnic, and fireworks. Everybody turned out for it. In 1845 Charles Sumner was the orator for Boston's celebration. War with Mexico was threatening and was actually welcomed by many people. The War of Independence, which had come to an end only sixty-three years earlier, was looked upon as sacred. At least a hundred men in the large and impressive audience that Sumner faced were wearing military or naval full-dress uniform. Charles Sumner spoke eloquently on peace, which he called "the true grandeur of nations." It was not a popular theme, and the uniformed gentlemen present, feeling personally insulted, were with difficulty prevented from walking out. Whittier later read the speech in its printed form and wrote Sumner an enthusiastic letter about it.

After that, Sumner, who was wholly opposed to slavery as well as to war, was much in demand for lectures at lyceums and antislavery meetings. In a speech before the American Peace Society in 1849 he pleaded for "a Congress of Nations with a High Court of Judicature" or, in modern terms, a League of Nations and a World Court. He also called the Mexican War "the most wicked act in our history." Again he was furiously criticized and some people declared him "outside the pale of Society."

The next year, after Daniel Webster had resigned from the Senate to become a member of President Fillmore's cabinet, the Free Soil Party, which had succeeded the Liberty Party, proposed that Charles Sumner run for Webster's place in the Senate as a Free Soil candidate. This idea did not at all appeal to Sumner, who was successful and contented on the Harvard Law faculty and who had never been drawn to politics anyhow. Whittier went to Phillips Beach, Swampscott, where Sumner was spending the summer, and had a long talk with him.

Reluctant at first, Sumner yielded to Whittier's persuasion. At that time United States senators were elected not by popular vote but by the state legislatures. There was a long struggle in the Massachusetts legislature among the Whigs, Democrats, and Free Soilers, but finally, in April 1851, Sumner won on the twenty-sixth ballot by a single vote. From then till the end of his life, he was re-elected senator from Massachusetts. Consultations, advice, meetings, and mutual admiration drew Whittier and Sumner together in a friendship that was important to both of them.

1854 was a crisis year. There were now in the Union thirty-one states, of which fifteen were slave and sixteen were free. The slave states were determined to keep the balance even. By the Missouri Compromise of 1820, all states above the 36° 30' latitude were to be free, all below it, slave—though Missouri itself, which was above the line, had been admitted as a slave state. Now two new territories, Kansas and Nebraska, both above the 36° 30' line, were waiting on the threshold for admission. If they came in as free states, the score would be fifteen to eighteen.

A group of Democrats in the Congress proposed to repeal the Missouri Compromise and pass what was called the Kansas-Nebraska Bill, by which settlers in the territories would themselves decide whether they would be slave or free. After three months of furious debate, the bill was passed. The North, already incensed by the Fugitive Slave Law, regarded the repeal of the Missouri Compromise as a betrayal. There were two immediate results.

One was the formation of a new party: the Republican, which grew out of the Free Soil Party, which in its turn had come from the Liberty Party. Because he had been one of the creators of the Liberty Party, Whittier always considered himself—and was so recognized by others—a founder of the Republican Party. It began at once to prepare for the presidential election of 1856.

The other result was that in order to get a majority in each territory, pro- and antislavery settlers from South and North poured into Kansas, determined and belligerent. Armed and bloody clashes occurred between the two factions, and the territory came to be known by the sorry name of "Bleeding Kansas."

Whittier wrote several stirring poems about the issue, one of which, "The Kansas Emigrants," was sung by a band of New Englanders as they made the long journey by covered wagon from Boston to Kansas.

> *We cross the prairie as of old*
> *The pilgrims crossed the sea*
> *To make the West as they the East*
> *The homestead of the free!*
>
> *We go to rear a wall of men,*
> *A Freedman's southern line*
> *And plant beside the cotton-tree*
> *The rugged Northern pine!*

In May 1856, Charles Sumner rose in the Senate and delivered a brilliant but inflammatory speech on "The Crime against Kansas," in which he attacked certain Southern senators by name. Preston S. Brooks, the cousin of one of them, came into the Senate chamber two days later at the end of the day. The room was deserted and Sumner was alone, clearing up his desk. Brooks lifted his heavy walking stick and beat the helpless Sumner into unconsciousness. He was seriously injured, and it was more than

Charles Sumner

John C. Frémont

three years before he was able to return to the Senate. It was the most brutal and disgraceful act ever to take place in the Senate of the United States. The country was outraged.

Whittier's sympathy and indignation were intense. As always, he did not seek retaliation or punishment but instead looked for a way to change the conditions that had caused the wrong. He wrote a letter to be read at a protest meeting of the inflamed and excited citizens of Amesbury—a letter, since he did not make speeches.

> The North is not united for freedom as the South is for slavery. We must forget, *forgive* and UNITE. . . . It is worse than folly to talk of fighting slavery when we have not yet agreed to vote against it. Our business is with poll-boxes, not cartridge-boxes; with ballots not bullets.

He had great hopes for the new Republican Party, which held its first national convention to nominate a president in Philadelphia that summer. The man nominated was the forty-five-year-old colorful John C. Frémont, soldier and explorer. He was best known for his daring expeditions into the Wind River chain of the Rocky Mountains and over the still little-mapped Oregon Trail. In the winter of 1845 he had made the first crossing of the High Sierra, a feat of great danger, coming down into California, which was then held by Mexico. For his part in the capture of California for the United States, when he acted contrary to orders, he was court-martialed on the charge of mutiny and disobedience, signal crimes for a soldier under orders. To the people as a whole, however, he was a romantic hero. President Polk remitted the penalty but Frémont indignantly resigned from the army.

His wife, Jessie, was the daughter of Thomas Hart Benton, a well-known and powerful senator from Missouri. She had eloped with Frémont when she was sixteen and he was twenty-eight. They had been forgiven by her father, who helped his exuberant son-in-law in many ways. Jessie herself had considerable literary skill, and it was owing to her help that the reports of Frémont's expeditions were so readable and so widely read.

Although he was born and reared in the South—or perhaps because of that fact—Frémont was an ardent abolitionist and Free Soiler. Whittier, the pacifist, who read the reports of his explorations with excitement and found his views on slavery admirable, was able to overlook his military exploits and to consider him an excellent candidate for president. Elizabeth Whittier was even more enthusiastic than her brother. She wrote to Lucy Larcom, begging her to write a campaign song for him, "Frémont is my hero of years; his wild ranger life has the greatest charm for me." Lucy did write a campaign song and Whittier wrote more than one. To Whittier also Frémont owed his campaign slogan: "Free Speech, Free Press, Free Soil, Free Men, Frémont and Victory."

One of the poems which Whittier wrote during the campaign was "The Pass of the Sierra," celebrating the struggle of Frémont's party in 1844 to cross the dangerous and then unknown High Sierra.

> Strong leader of that mountain band
> Another task remains
> To break from Slavery's desert land
> A path to Freedom's plains!
> . . .
>
> Rise up, Frémont! and go before;
> The Hour must have its Man;
> Put on the hunting shirt once more
> And lead in Freedom's van!

Jessie Frémont cut this poem out of the newspaper and pasted it on the wall beside her husband's shaving mirror where he could see it every day. But Frémont and Whittier were not to meet for some time to come. With the help of Southern votes, James Buchanan won the presidency in the election of 1856.

Before the next election year there occurred a tragic event that moved the already divided country closer to Civil War. John Brown, an antislavery settler from Kansas and veteran of the battles there, led a little band of thirteen white men and five Black men into Virginia to seize the U.S. Arsenal at Harpers Ferry. His idea was to create a haven for fugitive slaves in the mountains of Virginia. He was quickly captured, tried for treason, and hanged.

Some people in the North took up his act as a great cause to rally round. The South regarded it as a dangerous act of aggression against all the slave states. Whittier deplored the deed but sympathized with the man. "What a sad tragedy today in Virginia!" he wrote to a friend. "I feel deep sympathy for John Brown, but deplore from my heart his rash and insane attempt. It injures the cause he sought to serve."

He wrote a poem, "Brown of Ossawatamie," the theme of which was the transformation of hate into love. In the poem he tells how John Brown, on his way to the gallows, stooped and kissed the child of a Black slave held up to him. Actually Brown did stop and kiss a child, but it was the child of the white jailor. If Whittier had used the true story in his poem, it would have equally well brought out the significance of a loving gesture on the threshold of death, without outraging the feelings of many readers on both sides of the issue. The most disputed stanza read:

> *The shadows of his stormy life that moment fell apart;*
> *And they who blamed the bloody hand forgave the loving*
>   *heart.*
> *That kiss from all its guilty means redeemed the good in-*
>   *tent,*
> *And round the grisly fighter's hair the martyr's aureole*
>   *bent!*

The words *stormy, bloody, guilty, grisly* offended the radical abolitionists and supporters of John Brown. They thought that such words harmed the image of their man. Others were equally antagonized by the making of a hero out of a violent lawbreaker. In spite of criticism from both sides, the poem, printed in the *Independent* barely three weeks after Brown's execution, was immediately successful. It was much quoted and it had great influence, but not as Whittier intended. It helped to make of Brown a martyr and so aroused the warlike spirit that Whittier had hoped to allay.

When the Republican Convention met in the summer of 1860, Whittier hoped that Frémont would again be nominated. This time, however, the convention chose a not very well-known lawyer from Illinois named Abraham Lincoln. Whittier gave Lincoln his full support. Again he wrote campaign songs and poems. Pennsylvania was believed to be the state on which the election hung, and Whittier prophesied that the Society of Friends would cast the deciding votes. His vigorous campaign song was called, "The Quakers Are Out!" It had a fine catchy rhythm:

> *The good State had broken the cords for her spun;*
> *Her oil springs and water won't fuse into one;*
> *The Dutchman has seasoned with Freedom his kraut,*
> *And slow, late but certain the Quakers are out!*
>
> *Give the flags to the winds! set the hills all aflame!*
> *Make way for the man with the Patriarch's name!*
> *Away with misgiving, away with all doubt,*
> *For Lincoln goes in when the Quakers are out!*

When Pennsylvania voted for Lincoln in November, Whittier wrote to Lucy Larcom, "I agree with thee that hallelujah is better than hurra!" He was deeply relieved and thankful.

Several months later the electors from each state met to cast the actual ballot, and Whittier was a member of the Massachusetts Electoral College. When Lincoln was elected for the second time in 1864, Whittier proudly said that he was the only man who had been able to vote for him four times, twice at the polls and twice in the electoral college.

With Dr. Gamaliel Bailey's death in 1860 the *National Era* came to an end. There was no need to find another editor. Events had gone beyond the American and Foreign Anti-Slavery Society and its newspaper.

12. Friends-
and Especially
Elizabeth Lloyd

Even without Aunt Mercy Hussey, who had died in 1846, the little house in Amesbury was too cramped for the family of three adults, one of whom attracted an increasing number of visitors. With the help of a grant from Joseph Sturge, Whittier enlarged the house, extending the little room that had been Aunt Mercy's out into the garden and adding two more bedrooms on the second floor above it. The new room downstairs now became known as the Garden Room. Here the poet had his desk and his books and a comfortable chair before the open fire in the Franklin stove. Here the family gathered in the evenings, and here he entertained the guests who came, often from far away, to see him.

The garden itself, on which it opened, was a deep one with a grape arbor, fruit trees, and all the old-fashioned flowers—roses, sweet peas, sweet william, phlox—and a plot for vegetables. Once when Whittier was gathering grapes, two boys in the garden next door were practicing firing at a target. A bullet went wild and grazed his cheek. It bled copiously. Not wanting to frighten his mother, who was seventy-six, he clapped a handkerchief to his face and went off to get his doctor, who lived nearby, to put a patch on it. He said nothing to the boys, who heard what had happened only by chance some time later. Then one of them, in tears, came to Whittier and confessed. Whittier comforted him.

Elizabeth Whittier—or Lizzie, as she was called—had always been Whittier's pet in the family. Now the two were very close and dear companions. She supported and encouraged him in his abolitionism, admired and was proud of his poetry, read with him books that both enjoyed, helped him entertain the strangers who sought him out. Whereas he was shy, she was lively and outgoing. Her warmth and wit made her attractive to many people. She was a capable housekeeper and when the Quarterly Meeting met in May each year, the Friends came to Amesbury and were entertained at the Whittier house. Like Greenleaf, Lizzie was not strong, and his letters often contained an account of her state of health at the time of his writing. His friends were fond of her and interested in her.

A volume of his collected verse was issued in 1849 by a publisher named Hussey. It was handsomely bound in red and lettered in gold, with steel engravings of rural scenes to illustrate the poems. (Later his books were published by Tichnor and Fields and were bound like Longfellow's in dark blue and gold.) He wrote an introductory poem called "Proem," in which he spoke of his deficiencies as a poet. The metrical faults in his lines came, he said, from his "untaught ear"; their harshness he ascribed to haste and the storm and strife of his subjects. But his love of freedom was as deep and strong, he said, as Milton's or Marvell's, and he had

> *A hate of tyranny intense*
> *And hearty in its vehemence*
> *As if my brother's pain and sorrow were my own.*

Three years later James T. Fields brought out another volume of Whittier's poems, *Songs of Labor and Reform,* which con-

The Quaker Meeting House in Amesbury, built in 1851.
Whittier was chairman of the building committee

tained the poems about the shoemakers and drovers and lumbermen that had been published in the *National Era* and the *Democratic Review*. From now on Fields published all of Whittier's work, and he and his beautiful young wife Annie became two of Whittier's dearest friends.

Lucy Larcom came back from Illinois, where she had studied at the Monticello Female Seminary, to teach at Wheaton Seminary in Norton, Massachusetts, and she renewed her friendship with the Whittiers. She was nine years younger than Lizzie and though they were very close friends, the difference in age and Lucy's great respect for the Whittier family were enough, in those formal days, to make Lucy call Elizabeth "Aunt Lizzie," while Greenleaf was always Mr. Whittier to her. Lucy, now a large, motherly young woman and a successful teacher, became also a writer. When her first book of essays was ready, Whittier sent it to James Fields with a letter of recommendation, and it was published in 1854 with the title, *Similitudes from the Ocean and the Prairie*.

Another friend was Bayard Taylor, a young poet and novelist from Kennett Square, Pennsylvania. Their friendship had begun when Whittier praised Taylor's poem, "The Norseman's Ride," in the *National Era*. In a day when foreign travel was difficult, Taylor went not only to Europe and Scandinavia but to Africa, India, China, and even to Japan. He got himself attached to Commodore Perry's first expedition in 1853 as a member of the corps of artists and so was one of the first Americans to have a glimpse of Japan, which was then unknown and mysterious to the world outside. Whittier longed to travel but because of his frail health found even a trip to Philadelphia exhausting. He took delight in seeing distant places through Bayard Taylor's eyes. From time to time he arranged for Taylor to speak to the lyceum in Amesbury, and then he stayed overnight with the Whittiers.

"I travel a great deal by proxy," Whittier wrote to Taylor,

"I have had thee in my service for many years, very much to my satisfaction. Mr. Booth has been to Timbuctoo for me and Burton to Mexico. Atkinson has been doing Siberia for me. I think (if thy Marie does not object) of sending thee off again to find Xanadu and Kubla Khan." In his "The Last Walk in Autumn" he wrote of his pleasure in Taylor's travels:

> *Here too, of answering love secure,*
> *Have I not welcomed to my hearth*
> *The gentle pilgrim troubadour*
> *Whose songs have girdled half the earth;*
> *Whose pages, like the magic mat*
> *Whereon the eastern lover sat,*
> *Have borne over Rhineland's purple vines*
> *And Nubia's tawny sands and Phrygia's mountain pines!*

On one of Taylor's earliest visits to Whittier he was accompanied by James Russell Lowell, then just thirty-one, whose *Biglow Papers,* satirizing the Mexican War, were being widely read and quoted. They arrived in Amesbury in the midst of a northeast storm. Taylor wrote to a friend, "What a capital time we had with Whittier, in his nook of a study, with the rain pouring on the roof and the wind howling at the door!"

Even before his experience in Lowell and his friendship with Lucy Larcom, Whittier had been on the side of labor in its struggle to achieve a measure of justice in the new industrial society. He had in the *American Manufacturer* and in the *New England Review* advocated collective bargaining and the right to strike when these were new and radical ideas. In Amesbury in 1852 the mills opened at 5 A.M. and closed at 7 P.M. The workers had half an hour for breakfast and an hour for dinner; male workers could leave the mill for fifteen minutes in the morning and fifteen in the afternoon for "lunch." That left a working day of twelve hours. When a new manager came in and posted notices saying that the lunch privilege would be taken away, a hundred men left the mill in protest and were discharged. Whittier was present at the mass meeting of citizens that followed, and he drafted the resolutions that they adopted, calling for a ten-hour day.

The protest failed. The old workers who had left the mill were replaced by foreign immigrants, who accepted the conditions. But thirteen years later the ten-hour day at last became law.

Those years in the 1850s were difficult financially for Whittier. He and his mother and sister all suffered from ill health, and he had many medical bills to pay. He received very little money from the *National Era,* and the well-known literary magazines would not publish his poetry because of his reputation as an abolitionist. It is hard to believe now that less than five years before the Civil War the North was not united against slavery. True, all the eminent writers of the North had come out against it: Lowell, Longfellow, Emerson, Hawthorne, Harriet Beecher Stowe, as well as Whittier; but lawyers, clergymen, businessmen, and politicians either did not dare to commit themselves or were actually opposed to abolition. The national magazines, concerned about their circulation, generally avoided the subject, and writers known to be ardent abolitionists were not welcome in their pages. Whittier's friend, Lydia Maria Child, whose early novels had sold well, could not find a publisher for her later ones because of her vigorous *Appeal in Behalf of That Class of Americans Called Africans.* Those who did not have private means made up their incomes by traveling about and lecturing at lyceums. This recourse was not open to Whittier because of his shyness and ill health. In the year 1857, which was a depression year, generous Joseph Sturge offered help again and Whittier reluctantly accepted it. But relief was just over the horizon.

L. Maria Child.

In August Mr. Willard P. Phillips, a publisher in Boston, gave a dinner party attended by Whittier, Longfellow, Emerson, Motley, Holmes, and others. The purpose of the dinner was to plan a new magazine, which should offer an outlet to those writers who were banned from other publications. The magazine would be entertaining; it would welcome poetry, essays, and fiction, but in every issue there would also be one political article. Contributors were to be paid for their work. The name, the *Atlantic Monthly*, was suggested by Holmes, and Lowell was made editor in chief. So was born a magazine that for more than a century was to be of importance in American thought and to introduce a great number of brilliant new writers to the reading public. For Whittier it became an important source of income, and it established his position as a writer of more than antislavery poems. Lowell, who had been the first of the Boston Brahmins to recognize Whittier's stature, was an encouraging and sympathetic editor, and when, after five years, he retired, he was succeeded by Whittier's friend, James T. Fields.

From now on Whittier's poems were to appear regularly in the *Atlantic Monthly*. The first was a narrative poem called "The Gift of Tritemius," the tale of a bishop who gave the silver candlesticks from the altar to a man in need and found them miraculously replaced by gold ones. It was soon followed by the fine ballad, "Skipper Ireson's Ride" and later by "Telling the Bees." This was perhaps Whittier's best short lyric and indeed a perfect poem of its type. It is based on an old tradition that when a member of a family dies, the bees must be told or they will go and hive somewhere else. In the poem a young man comes after a month's absence to see the girl he loves, and as he approaches the farmhouse (which is the farmhouse of Whittier's boyhood) he sees the "chore-girl small" draping each beehive with a bit of black crepe and "drearily singing." The stanzas are simple and poignant.

Trembling I listened; the summer sun
  Had the chill of snow;
For I knew she was telling the bees of one
  Gone on the journey we all must go!

Then I said to myself, "My Mary weeps
  For the dead today;
Haply her old blind grandsire sleeps
  The fret and the pain of his age away."

But then he sees the old man sitting in the doorway with his chin
propped on his cane, and the chore-girl goes on singing.

And the song she was singing ever since
  In my ear sounds on:—
"Stay at home, pretty bees, fly not hence!
  Mistress Mary is dead and gone!"

Many of his poems Whittier spoiled, for present-day taste,
by tacking on a moral, but he left this one to bring its message of
love and sorrow without any comment of his own.

In 1858 Whittier's mother died, a sore loss for him and for
Lizzie. She had been the heart of their household. In the same year
Joseph Sturge, who had been one of England's great philan-
thropists as well as Whittier's friend, also died. Whittier wrote of
him:

The gentlest of all human natures
  He joined to courage strong
And love outreaching unto all God's creatures
  With sturdy hate of wrong.

The year 1858 was also the year in which he and Elizabeth
Lloyd, the most beautiful and interesting of the four Elizabeths of

his *Pennsylvania Freeman* days, began to see each other again and to correspond.

In 1853 she had married Robert Howell of Philadelphia, who was not a member of the Society of Friends. Their marriage was a happy one, tragically ended by her husband's death from smallpox in 1856. For two years she was prostrated with grief, and then she and Whittier, each sympathizing with the other's sorrow, hers for her husband, his for his mother and for Joseph Sturge, began to write to each other and from time to time to see each other, when he visited Philadelphia or she came to New England.

The following spring, when Elizabeth was forty-eight and he nearly fifty-two, he spent three weeks in Philadelphia, staying at the fashionable Girard House and seeing Elizabeth frequently. On his return to Amesbury, he wrote to her:

> Elizabeth, I have been happy—far more than I ever expected in this life. The sweet memory of the past few weeks makes me rich forever. What Providence has in store for the future I know not—I dare not hope scarcely—but the past is mine—may I not say ours—sacred and beautiful, a joy forever. Asking nothing of thee and with the tenderest regards for thy griefs and memories I have given thee what was thine by right—the love of an honest heart—not as a restraint or burden upon thee, imposing no obligation and calling for no solicitation on thy part as regards myself. Nobody is the loser by loving or being loved.

Some have thought on the strength of this letter that they were engaged to be married, but if they were it was only tentative and it did not last long. She went to Elmira, New York, to take the "water cure," fashionable then for those who could afford it as a treatment for almost any ill. Presumably Elizabeth's eyes were troubling her, for Whittier urged her not to write to him if her eyes hurt, "for the very blank pages which thy hand has folded will be dear to me for thy sake."

For the next three months letters flew back and forth between them at the rate of one or two and occasionally three a week. She sent him her miniature, he signed himself to her, "Ever and truly thine." It seems as if they were moving toward a marriage that offered a rich companionship for both, but something happened that summer.

Elizabeth Howell had become critical of Quakerism, but her attitude does not seem to have troubled Whittier seriously. He wrote her on July 9 from Boston, where he had gone for an *Atlantic* dinner, "Heart and soul I am a Quaker and, as respects forms, rituals, priests and churches, unsparing as Milton or John Knox. I don't see any saving virtue in candles, surplices, altars and prayer books. At the same time I am but an indifferently good Quaker—I take my own way and Friends theirs. I don't see how I could be any more free."

Lizzie was not well that summer. On July 14, Whittier wrote that she was in a "deep depression." He did not say what was troubling her, but it may well have been that she dreaded having her life changed by the marriage of the brother whom she so deeply loved and on whom she was dependent—and to a woman as brilliant, as well-to-do, and as worldly as Elizabeth Howell had become.

Elizabeth Howell evidently felt a difference in Whittier's letters and asked him about it, for on August 3 he was writing her, "If there has been any change in the letters I am sure there is no change in the feeling which dictated them as far as *thou* art concerned." But he was questioning himself and his ability to make those he loved happy. He saw a great difference between his own "old-fashioned and homely" ways and her life of "fashion and society." He was "constantly baffled by illness and weakness";

he felt that her "fine artist nature would pine and die under the hard and uncongenial influences" that made him what he was and which he could not escape without abandoning his duty. "There seems at times a wide space between us, which I feel I have no power or right even to cross. . . . Dear sister is not, I think, any better. She cannot walk out much nor ride without making her worse and she has many cares which weigh upon her and depress her."

They continued to write to each other, even though it was now tacitly recognized that their friendship would not grow into a deeper relationship. He himself became seriously ill early in 1860, and she was much concerned about him. Later in the year he went to see her in Princeton, where she lived after her return from Elmira, and she visited the Whittiers in Amesbury. He wrote to her after Lincoln's election, "Lincoln is a very conservative, cautious and moderate man and will do nothing rash or illegal. . . . God grant that this awful question of slavery may have a peaceful solution!"

After a time she evidently asked him to burn her letters to him, for he replied, "I have obliged thee as to thy letters—reluctantly but with a feeling that thee has a right to their disposal."

After the Civil War, when Whittier sent her a copy of his *Snow-Bound,* Elizabeth Howell wrote that she was thinking of going to England. Later she wrote him from London, "I have a charming circle of English friends."

Years later he told his cousin, Gertrude Whittier Cartland, that Elizabeth Lloyd was the only woman he had ever loved, but that marriage had been impossible because he had had his mother and sister to support. By the time that they parted, his mother had died and his financial situation was easier. It seems more likely that the opportunity to marry had just come too late. His health was too precarious; he had been too long a bachelor; the claims of habit and his affection for his sister bound him to his narrow life in Amesbury.

13. "It Is Done!"

For much of the North—perhaps most of the North—slavery was not the main issue in the Civil War; union was. For Whittier and others like him, the issue was slavery. If it could have been *"the* Union of our fathers," he said, he would have liked to preserve it, but "as to fighting, in any event, to *force back* the seceders, I see no sense in it. Let them go with their mad experiment."

From the depths of his being he hated war, but when it actually came he was torn with conflict. If the North won, slavery would be abolished. He longed for the result but he loathed the means, more and more deeply as the horror of the struggle unfolded itself. "The shadow of this terrible war lies heavily on me," he wrote, and yet he was "excited by its heroism and opportunity."

To the Society of Friends he wrote a circular letter. "Our mission is at this time to mitigate the sufferings of our countrymen, to visit and aid the sick and wounded, to relieve the necessities of the widow and orphan and to practise economy for the sake of charity."

Frémont, who had returned to the army, was now a general, behaving in the same impulsive way that had got him into trouble before. Having won a victory over guerrillas in Missouri, he issued a proclamation declaring the property of the Missouri rebels confiscated and their slaves freed. It was premature and unauthorized. Lincoln removed Frémont from his command.

Whittier, sympathizing with Frémont's freeing of the slaves, wrote a poem to him beginning:

> *Thy error, Frémont, simply was to act*
> *A brave man's part without the statesman's tact.*

The Emancipation Proclamation, when it came in 1862 after the Battle of Antietam, was a political move. It applied only to the Confederate states, not to Missouri, Kentucky, Maryland, and Delaware, which remained slave states. "The emancipation that came by military necessity and enforced by bayonets," Whittier wrote, "was not the emancipation for which we worked and prayed."

He believed moreover that emancipation was not enough; it was only the beginning. The slaves suddenly thrust into freedom needed education for their new life and opportunities to earn their living. He wrote to William Lloyd Garrison of the responsibility

> to aid, direct and educate these millions left free indeed but bewildered, ignorant, naked and foodless in the wild chaos of civil war. We have to undo the accumulated wrongs of two centuries and to remake the manhood which slavery has well-nigh unmade; to see to it that the oppressed colored man has a fair field for development and improvement and to tread under our feet the last vestige of that hateful prejudice which has been the strongest external support of Southern slavery.

As the war rolled on, gathering to itself the corruption that war always does, the profiteering, the maneuvering for power, Whittier suffered. He wrote to Lucy Larcom in 1863:

> God only knows whether we really deserve success in this terrible war. When I think of the rapacity of contractors and office holders and of the brutal and ferocious prejudice against the poor blacks. . . . I almost despair, so far as we, the whites of the North, are concerned. God's will be done, whatever becomes of us.

That summer Lucy Larcom, Whittier, and Elizabeth went together to Appledore in the Isles of Shoals for a holiday. Celia Thaxter, the poet and novelist, and her family kept a hotel on one of those windswept, wave-tossed islands off the coast of New Hampshire from Portsmouth. A great many interesting and well-known people came to it, to walk on the long porch of the inn or sit in its rocking chairs, to enjoy the garden and the rocks and the fresh sea air. In the cool evenings around the open fire the talk was stimulating and often brilliant. It should have been a delightful and refreshing time for all three of them, but Elizabeth fell on the rocks and suffered an injury to her spine from which she never fully recovered.

In spite of his dislike of the war, Whittier also saw its gallant actions and the heroism it evoked. He wrote poems that lifted the spirits of people in the North or deepened their dedication to freedom. One was the famous "Barbara Frietchie."

Mrs. E. D. E. N. Southworth, a popular novelist whom Whittier had met when he was corresponding editor of the *National Era,* sent him a story that she had heard from a relative of the old woman who was its heroine. He retold it in ballad form, and it was published in the *Atlantic Monthly.*

Up from the meadows rich with corn
Clear in the cool September morn

The clustered spires of Frederick stand
Green walled by the hills of Maryland.

The Union flags were flying, but as Stonewall Jackson and
his troops approached, the flags were all cautiously taken in, until
only one still waved from the attic window of ninety-year-old Barbara Frietchie. General Jackson ordered his men to fire on it. As
the staff was shattered, Barbara caught the flag, leaned out of the
window

And shook it forth with a royal will.

"Shoot if you must this old gray head
But spare your country's flag," she said.

The nobler nature within him stirred
To life at that woman's deed and word.

"Who touches a hair of yon gray head
Dies like a dog! March on!" he said.

The ballad with its dramatic, easy-to-remember lines and
its sentimental appeal swept the country. It was reprinted, recited,
quoted, parodied. Here and there letters appeared in newspapers
saying that it had not really happened just that way, that actually
two flags had flown in Frederick that morning. But no one minded,
Whittier least of all. It was a ballad and it reached people's hearts.
With Julia Ward Howe's "Battle Hymn of the Republic" and
Walt Whitman's great poem on Lincoln, "O Captain! My
Captain!" it was one of the three most read and best-loved poems
of the Civil War.

Another of Whittier's poems that had a far-reaching effect

was a hymn, which was set to the solemn and moving music of Luther's hymn "A Mighty Fortress Is Our God."

> *We wait beneath the furnace blast*
> *The pangs of transformation;*
> *Not painlessly does God recast*
> *And mould anew the nation.*
> *Hot burns the fire*
> *Where wrongs expire;*
> *Nor spares the hand*
> *That from the land*
> *Uproots the ancient evil.*

This too, in a deeper way, stirred the country. Lincoln read it to his cabinet, it was sung in churches and homes and army camps.

These and other poems of this period were gathered together and published by James T. Fields in a little volume called *In War Time*. A poem not included in the book was a Christmas hymn that Whittier wrote at the request of his friend Charlotte Forten, to be sung by her Black pupils on St. Helena Island near Charleston, South Carolina.

Years before, Whittier had written a poem "To the Daughters of James Forten." Charlotte was a granddaughter of James Forten, who had been a Black shipbuilder in Philadelphia and had served in the Revolution. He was seventy when Whittier first met him in Philadelphia at the convention of the American Anti-Slavery Society. Charlotte, who was born in 1837, had been educated in Salem, Massachusetts, where schools were not segregated. On her return to Philadelphia she was shocked by the Jim Crow laws and went back to Salem as a teacher.

Because of these friendships with Blacks of intellectual capacity and personal charm, Whittier was able as few were in his time to meet them as individual human beings first and members of another race later. He was thus preserved from the condescension, conscious or unconscious, that often infected the relationship between white abolitionists and the people whom they gave so much of their energy to help.

Charlotte had visited the Whittiers in Amesbury, and Whittier advised her to apply for the job of teaching the children on St. Helena Island, who had been freed when the island was taken over by Northern troops. She wrote Whittier delightful letters about life on the island, which he sent to the *Atlantic Monthly*. They were published in May and June 1864. Whittier wrote to her in May, "We have had a cold spring and still the dreadful east winds blow and sing their harsh discords among the appleblossoms. It is Quarterly Meeting today and our house is over-run with drab-colored people. I enclose a sprig of may-flower from our woods."

Whittier was a devoted Quaker but he could not resist making fun of Quakers sometimes—and criticizing them too, for their narrowness, their coldness, their plain speaking, which now and then "deteriorated into rude speaking," and their "uncouthness of apparel." Though he was himself color-blind and could not see red or green, he delighted in yellows, bronzes, and blues, and he had a discriminating eye for clothes.

In the summer of 1863 Jessie Benton Frémont and her daughter came to see Whittier from Nahant, where they had a cottage. She remembered that visit vividly thirty years later and described it in detail. She did not tell Whittier at first who she was, but led up to it with a story of her husband: how he had been dejected, lonely, suffering, how she had read to him a poem of Whittier's that she had found in the newspaper.

He was speechless with increasing, overwhelming feeling—transfigured. Taking the paper and bending to read it for himself by the blazing logs, at length he said,

"He speaks for posterity. I *knew* I was right. I want these words on my tombstone:—

God has spoken through thee
Irrevocable, the mighty words, Be Free!

Whittier had grasped my arm and his eyes blazed. "What is thy name?"

"Frémont."

Without a word he swung out of the room, to return, infolding in his helping embrace a frail little woman, tenderly saying to the invalid he was bringing from her seclusion—

"Elizabeth, this is Jessie Frémont—under our roof. Our mother would have been glad to see this day!"

The following summer Whittier and Jessie Frémont met again.

The time for another presidential election had come. Before the Republican Convention took place in Philadelphia, a number of western Germans, radicals, and "War Democrats" met in Cleveland and nominated Frémont. The chairman of the Republican Party asked Frémont to withdraw, but he was reluctant to do so. If Frémont ran for president, the Republican Party would be split, and Lincoln would almost certainly have been defeated just when he was most needed.

Whittier left the bedside of Elizabeth, who was now seriously ill, and went to Nahant to talk with Frémont himself at his cottage there.

"There is a time to *do*," he told the man whom he had so long admired, "and a time to *stand aside*."

Frémont heeded him. Years later Jessie Frémont wrote to Whittier, "It was a deciding word, coming from you." Lincoln was elected by a substantial majority.

In September of that year, Elizabeth Whittier died after months of pain and weariness. For many years she had been

Elizabeth Whittier

Greenleaf's beloved companion. Now he was alone in the house where once he had had three devoted women to cherish him: his Aunt Mercy, his mother, his sister Elizabeth. His elder sister, Mary Caldwell, who lived in Haverhill, had died four years earlier. His brother Frank by this time had moved from Portland to Boston, where he had a post in the Customs House. Now he and Greenleaf were the last of the family.

Frank's daughter, Lizzie, who had lived with her aunt and uncle in Amesbury for several years, took over the housekeeping for Whittier after Elizabeth died. Sometimes her younger sister Alice was there too.

On January 31, 1865, the Thirteenth Amendment to the Constitution, abolishing slavery, was adopted by the Congress of the United States. Now it was binding on the whole country. Whittier was at a Thursday morning meeting for worship when the news came, and the whole town of Amesbury exploded in joyous bell-ringing and the firing of cannon. The Friends continued their meeting in silence, but Whittier's mind was busy. Line by line, stanza by stanza, a poem came to him, bearing in its rhythms the peal and clang of the bells themselves. When he reached home he recited it to his niece in the garden room. He called it "Laus Deo."

> *It is done!*
> *Clang of bell and roar of gun*
> *Send the tidings up and down!*
> *How the belfries rock and reel!*
> *How the great guns peal on peal*
> *Fling the joy from town to town!*

He was too modest to take any credit to himself for this great event, but R. C. Waterston, president of the Massachusetts Historical Society, wrote to him:

"You have done all that a human being could to bring it

about. Perhaps you do not know how much, for those words which you have given to the country have given impulse to who can say how many hearts. They have stirred the Conscience. They have strengthened Faith. They have awakened Zeal. . . . They have helped—greatly—to remould the Nation.''

The Civil War came to an end at last in April 1865, and a week later Lincoln was assassinated. Whittier, who wrote so many poems in memory of men and women whom he had loved and admired, was too shaken to write about Lincoln in public. To a friend he wrote:

''The assassination of the President has painfully affected me. I have hardly been able since to collect my thoughts, to fathom the extent of our loss or to forecast the consequences. I bow, humbled and awed, before the mysterious providence.''

14. Snow-Bound

As editor of the *Atlantic Monthly* Lowell had written to Whittier, "I shall not let you rest till I have got a New England pastoral out of you." Whittier replied, "The pastoral shall be thought of."

The summer of 1865 found Whittier feeling lonely and ill. Elizabeth was gone. The slaves were free. Though he was deeply concerned about Reconstruction in the South and about healing the wounds of war, his own active political life was over. He was almost sixty. He had a number of volumes of poems behind him, including a *Collected Poems* bound in blue and gold in the same format as poems by Longfellow and Lowell. But he had not yet written anything that absorbed his entire creative energy. His mind went back to his boyhood and the life on the farm.

"I am writing a poem, 'Snow-Bound, a Winter Idyl,' a homely picture of old New England homes," he wrote to James Fields. "If I ever finish it I hope and trust it will be good."

This was August 28. The poem moved swiftly, as if it had been long waiting to emerge from the hidden recesses of his mind. On the third of October he sent a manuscript to Fields. It was published as a book four months later.

It is a perfect example of its type, the idyl or pastoral.
There are not many idyls in American poetry and no other that sur-
passes this picture of New England life. Only Robert Frost has
been able to express the essence of New England with the understanding that Whittier showed in this poem. Other poems by Whittier may be dated by their theme or language or rhythms; this is
timeless.

It consists of 759 lines, rhymed for the most part in pairs. It
is a picture of Whittier's own family and the farm on which he
grew up, during the week of a snowstorm that cut them off from
the rest of the world. It is full of the contrasts that give life its tension, depth, and color: the contrast between the cold outside and
the fire within the house; between the warmth of love and the chill
of death; the isolation of the storm and the return to the world; the
action of the storm and the poet's reflections.

It begins with a vivid picture of the coming of the storm:

The sun that brief December day
Rose cheerless over hills of gray
And, darkly circled, gave at noon
A sadder light than waning moon.

All day and all night and all the next day, the snow fell. On
the second morning,

We looked upon a world unknown,
On nothing we could call our own. . . .
No cloud above, no earth below,—
A universe of sky and snow!

The barn with its hungry stock was cut off from the house.
Into the stillness, action bursts:

A prompt, decisive man, no breath
Our father wasted: "Boys, a path!"

That evening the family and its guests, who were storm-bound with them, sat around the blazing hearth, whose fire was reflected in the window as if it burned on the snow outside.

While radiant with a mimic flame
Outside the sparkling drift became,
And through the bare-boughed lilac tree
Our own warm hearth seemed blazing free.

On the hearth a mug of cider simmered, apples were set to roast, a basket full of nuts from their own wood stood ready. And now the poet paused to think of the changes that had come over the years; how he and his brother, to whom the poem was dedicated, were the only ones of all the family left. He thinks of life after death.

Yet Love will dream and Faith will trust
(Since He who knows our needs is just)
That somehow, somewhere, meet we must.

They sit before the fire and tell stories; each member of the family is described directly and also indirectly by the kind of story he told, which showed his interests. Whittier's father told of his early adventures going on foot through the forest to Canada. The mother, spinning or knitting as she spoke, for her hands were never idle, told legends of the country along the Piscataqua where she grew up and tales of early heroic Quakers.

Our uncle, innocent of books,
Was rich in lore of fields and brooks.

Then came Aunt Mary,

> *The sweetest woman ever Fate*
> *Perverse denied a household mate,*

who told of country pleasures, sleigh rides, sailing, husking bees.
The kind and honest elder sister came next, and then

> *Upon the motley-braided mat*
> *Our youngest and our dearest sat,*
> *Lifting her large, sweet, asking eyes.*

The poem is again interrupted, and its mood deepened by
Whittier's reflections on Elizabeth and their love for each other,
seen not against the snowy night but on their walks together in the
fields of June. He pictures her waiting for him at the gates of sunset.

The schoolteacher came next,

> *Large-brained, clear-eyed, of such as he*
> *Shall Freedom's young apostles be,*
> *Who, following in War's bloody trail*
> *Shall every lingering wrong assail;*
> *All chains from limb and spirit strike,*
> *Uplift the black and white alike.*

There was one other guest caught in the storm, an eccentric
woman named Harriet Livermore, daughter of a New Hampshire
judge.

> *A not unfeared, half-welcome guest,*
> *Rebuking with her cultured phrase*
> *Our homeliness of words and ways.*

She went about the United States and Europe and even as far as Smyrna and Jerusalem, preaching the second coming of Christ; she was well known in her day. If Whittier is ever supposed to be invariably gentle, readers should turn to this picture of Harriet Livermore, which was etched in acid, "as near the life," he wrote, "as I can give it." He makes us see her dazzling teeth, her low brows, black as night, the eyes lit "with a dangerous light," in short,

> *A woman tropical, intense*
> *In thought and act, in soul and sense,*
> *She blended in a like degree*
> *The vixen and the devotee.*

But, he went on compassionately, we do not know

> *What forged her cruel chain of moods,*
> *What set her feet in solitudes,*
>   *And held the love within her mute.*

The contrast between this stormy figure and the gentle members of the family is another one of the webs of opposites that make the strong fabric of the poem.

The next day the ox teams came through, opening the deeply drifted roads; the doctor came by to ask Mrs. Whittier to go to the aid of a sick neighbor; the weekly newspaper arrived,

> *And all the world was ours once more!*

The poem ends as the poet himself turns from the memories of the past to the larger hopes and fears of the time that lies before him. He thinks that perhaps some of his readers may turn back to their own boyhoods and that his old friends who are still living may

> *pause to view*
> *These Flemish pictures of old days.*

The Flemish painters were famous for their small, vivid, accurate pictures of ordinary life; it was an apt comparison for the word pictures that he drew in his poem.

Snow-Bound was immediately popular. The time was right for it. People were tired of war and sad about the state of the country; they were glad to look back upon a simpler, sweeter day. The beauty and power of the writing gave the poem authority. From the first edition Whittier received $10,000—and more editions were to come later. For the first time in his life—when his mother and sister were no longer there to benefit from it—he knew relief from financial pressure. He sent his niece Lizzie away to boarding school, to Ipswich Seminary, and while she was away a Scottish housekeeper named Margaret took care of him.

Even before the success of *Snow-Bound*, Whittier had suffered some of the inconveniences of being a well-known figure: people asking for autographs and letters and poems, people coming to see him unannounced, intruding into his home, interrupting his day. Now he was overwhelmed. He wrote to Lucy Larcom:

"I have had a great many strangers coming to look at me and make speeches to me. It's a sort of thing to make one feel sadly mean and ridiculous. . . . I would rather chop wood than talk poetry with strangers."

If there happened to be a convention in town, he knew that many of the members would try to fill the empty spaces in their day with a visit to him, and he would escape into his pear orchard behind the house and hide until they had gone. But he did not avoid all strangers, only those who embarrassed him by their silliness or persistence. Mrs. Fields tells a pleasant story of his encounter with one lonely foreigner.

It was a hot summer day in Amesbury, with the terrible

dust that blanketed town and country before blacktop roads. A circus had come to the village. Whittier, walking in his garden, saw a slender, dark young man lean against his gate, reading from a small book. Curious, as all bookworms are, to see what the book was, he went to speak to the young man and learned that he was an Arab from the circus, desperately homesick for the desert with its sand and palms. The book he was reading was the Koran. Whittier, who had read most of the sacred books of most of the religions of the world, knew the Koran well. The Arab was delighted to be welcomed in this strange country by the kindly man who could talk with him about his bible.

Two years after *Snow-Bound* had appeared, Annie Fields was raising money for the education of freedmen by getting well-known poets to come and read their poems to people who paid for the privilege of listening. Bryant was hesitating, but would agree to do it if Whittier would. She asked Whittier. He wrote back:

"Thee ask a miracle of me. Anything within the bounds of my possibilities I would do, as thee very well know, not only for the cause's sake but for thine. Ask me to dance the polka or walk a slack rope from the Bank Street steeple to the State House dome—but don't ask me to read my rhymes to a Boston audience."

As a young man he had longed for fame; now he found that

Even fame itself may come to be
But wearying notoriety.

15. The Wood-Thrush
of Essex

Two years after *Snow-Bound* Whittier again produced a best seller, *The Tent on the Beach*. Collections of story-telling poems in a frame have been popular ever since Boccaccio pictured a group of Italians, driven out of fourteenth-century Florence by the plague, who passed the time by telling stories, and Chaucer had his pilgrims tell their tales along the road to Canterbury. Four years earlier Longfellow had made the inn at South Sudbury famous with his popular *Tales of a Wayside Inn*. Whittier, to vary the pattern, had one man read a series of poems to two others.

The scene was Salisbury Beach, not far from Amesbury, then empty, lonely, and beautiful, with a view of Rivermouth Rocks and on clear days of the Isles of Shoals, where Whittier's friend Celia Thaxter ran her hotel, wrote poetry, and cared for her flowers.

Three friends, the poet himself, James Fields, the editor, and Bayard Taylor, the traveler, pitched a tent on the beach and spent a few days there, fishing, watching boats pass, talking, dreaming, listening to the poet's tales and commenting on them.

The poet described himself in these words:

And one there was, a dreamer born,
  Who with a mission to fulfill
Had left the Muses' haunts to turn
  The crank of an opinion mill,
Making his rustic reed of song
A weapon in the war with wrong.

"The Wreck of Rivermouth" was the first tale in the book, a ballad in which Whittier retold an old legend of the neighborhood. In the seventeenth century a boat full of young people sailed out from Hampton, was cursed by an old woman reputed to be a witch, and was wrecked in a sudden storm on Rivermouth Rocks. It was characteristic of Whittier that he made the supposed witch wonder whether her words had caused the tragedy.

"They are lost!" she muttered, "boat and crew!
Lord forgive me if my words were true!"

Between tales the three friends talked about poetry itself, and Whittier set forth his conviction that there was a place for a message in a poem. He had the traveler bring up the principle of art for art's sake.

Art no other saction needs
Than beauty for its own dear sake.

(That art could also find its integrity in ugliness was not even imagined at that time.) But Whittier, the traveler charged, was not willing merely to tell a story.

You check the free play of your rhymes to clap
A moral underneath, then close it like a trap.

Though he recognized the esthetic point of view and could make fun of himself and the moral that he often tacked on to his tales, Whittier defended his belief that poetry had something positive and helpful to say to its readers and an interpretation as well as a picture to give.

> *The liberal range of Art should be*
> *The breadth of Christian liberty. . . .*
> *He wisest is who only gives,*
> *True to himself, the best he can.*

Among the poems was one called "The Cable Hymn." The trans-Atlantic cable had just been completed; for the first time in history instant communication between Europe and America was possible. This was as great a wonder in its day as the first man on the moon in ours, and Whittier like many others hoped that the end of war would be near when

> *Round the world the thought of all*
> *Is as the thought of one.*

Before he read "Abraham Davenport," which was the best poem in the book and one of the best of all Whittier's poems, the poet admitted that it had a hint

> *Of the old preaching mood in it*
> *The sort of sidelong moral squint*
> *Our friend objects to.*

But the moral this time was in the story itself, and the poem was written with economy of words and a touch of irony.

In the old days (a custom laid aside
With breeches and cocked hats) the people sent
Their wisest men to make the public laws.

On May 1, 1780, an eclipse of the sun had occurred. The terrified members of the Connecticut legislature, thinking the end of the world was at hand, decided they had better adjourn at once. But Abraham Davenport said sturdily:

"Let God do His work, we will see to ours.
Bring in the candles." And they brought them in.

In contrast to the solemnity of the atmosphere, the work they had to do was trivial: to revise the laws on shad and alewife fishery. But Abraham Davenport spoke well on the subject. He was, the poem concluded:

A witness to the ages as they pass
That simple duty hath no place for fear.

When *The Tent on the Beach* was published, it was an immediate success, selling at the rate of a thousand copies a day. With *Snow-Bound*, it established Whittier as one of the best-loved poets of his period. Ironically, now that he was sixty and alone, worldly success came to him. Though he was generous in his help to those in need, he lived simply, and when he died he left a small fortune.

The following year he published *Among the Hills and Other Poems*. The title poem was a long, romantic tale of a simple farmer in the Sandwich Mountains of New Hampshire, whose marriage to a lovely young woman of the city was happy and successful. More interesting than the poem itself was its "Prelude," which contained a vivid description of that beautiful countryside in brooding summer heat and also, surprisingly, a grim picture of another aspect of country life, of what we now term rural slums. Not often did Whittier write with such bitter realism. He knew, he said,

Too well the picture has another side.

He listed the grind of toil, the old homesteads blistering in the sun, with weeds around the door, the rags of shiftlessness fluttering at the curtainless windows, the cluttered kitchen floor, the piled-up rubbish at the chimney's back,

And in keeping with all things about them,
Shrill, querulous women, sour and sullen men,
Untidy, loveless, old before their time,
With scarce a human interest save their own
Monotonous round of small economies
Or the poor scandal of the neighborhood.

They were churchgoers, he said, but they begrudged the money that it cost to support the church; they had no understanding of Christian charity in daily life.

Saving, as shrewd economists, their souls
And winter pork with the least possible outlay
Of salt and sanctity.

This poem, like a number of others, came out of summers spent in New Hampshire. For many years he went to Ossipee, under the mountain now called Mt. Whittier in his honor, and beside the swift-running stream called Bear-Camp Water. In Center Sandwich, Center Harbor, Holderness, and Intervale there were also pleasant country inns in which he liked to stay. Friends would come and join him there, his cousins, Joseph and Gertrude Cartland, his nieces, Lucy Larcom, and others, and he had always an affectionate and admiring circle around his chair on the inn porch or beside the fieldstone fireplace on chilly evenings. A master storyteller, he had a hearty laugh and a habit of slapping his thigh when amused. "I like it hugely!" he would exclaim when something delighted him. There was no generation gap where he was concerned; young people loved to be with him.

At Bear-Camp House one day a young woman said to him, "Mr. Whittier, you never wrote a love song. I do not believe you *can* write one. I would like to have you try to write one for me."

The next day he gave her "The Henchman," a delicate lyric suggesting the period of knights and ladies and the unreturned love of a humble young man.

> *My lady walks her morning round,*
> *My lady's page her fleet greyhound,*
> *My lady's hair the fond winds stir,*
> *And all the birds make songs for her. . . .*
>
> *The distance of the stars is hers;*
> *The least of all her worshippers,*
> *The dust beneath her dainty heel,*
> *She knows not that I see or feel.*

One of the liveliest of his women friends was Mary Abigail Dodge, a clever and successful journalist well known under the pen name Gail Hamilton. Twenty-six years younger than Whittier, she adopted a playful, exaggeratedly admiring tone with him that delighted and occasionally startled him. "Dearly beloved," her letters would begin, or "Dear angel," or sometimes, "My dear Sheikh." During the Civil War she crocheted for him a pair of slippers decorated with the American eagle belligerently clutching thunderbolts in his claws, but worked in Quaker drab, a tacit gibe at the conflict within him between his pacifism and his desire for the North to win the war. He saw the joke and pointed it out to guests to whom he lent the slippers.

"Don't say you have a cold," she told him once when she sent him an invitation. "You always have a cold."

His letters to her were affectionate and amused. Thanking her for the gift of her newest book, he wrote that he quarreled with it often, but that he would not put quarrels on paper. "I will simply say that my old bachelor reverence for women has been somewhat disturbed by thy revelations." But in a poem, "Lines on a Flyleaf," he praised another book of hers.

> *It may be* [he conceded] *that she wields a pen*
> *Too sharply nibbed for thin-skinned men,*

but he found on her pages

> *Electric words in which I find*
> *The tonic of the northwest wind,*

and he counted her among the little group of brave women who had raised their voices against slavery: Lydia Maria Child, Anne E. Dickinson, Grace Greenwood, and Harriet Beecher Stowe.

His friendships were not all with women. Lowell, Longfellow, Holmes, and Emerson were also among his friends. "Emerson," he wrote after Emerson's death, "was a delightful companion and was often here. No matter who remained, when he left there was always a void." It was Emerson who lent him the Bhagavad-Gita, sometimes called the New Testament of Hinduism, and they must have had many talks about their common interest in Eastern religion. Whittier, though a Christian, was never narrowly or exclusively so. To him the quality of a man's life was more important than his beliefs.

The Garden Room

Call him not heretic whose works attest
His faith in goodness by no creed confessed.

His old friend Charles Sumner died in 1873. After the Civil War was over, they disagreed about the Republican Party, which Sumner left and to which Whittier remained loyal. Whittier moreover could not approve of all Sumner's actions in the Senate, but in spite of their disagreements they continued to be friends. After Sumner's death Whittier wrote a fine poem about him. He admitted his friend's defects, his pride, his overzealousness, his lack of humor, while reminding people, who had largely forgotten, of Sumner's courage, his compassion, his honesty, his unwavering championship of the cause of freedom.

Visiting foreigners sought Whittier out: Charles Kingsley, author of *The Water Babies;* the poet Matthew Arnold; George Macdonald, the Scottish minister, who wrote *At the Back of the North Wind* and *The Princess and Purdie,* as well as a number of novels. Of their visit to Amesbury Mrs. Macdonald wrote:

"Mr. Whittier's house is a sweet, country-like cottage, wooden and low. We dined in the room that the roadside door opened on. Then, through that was the little, sacred study for one of the sweetest, most dignified, loving, humble and gentle of men. . . . He is full of fire and enjoyment of all things good. He is very wide in his beliefs."

Dom Pedro, the scholarly and enlightened emperor of Brazil, had discovered Whittier's poetry in 1855 and after that got each volume as it came out. He visited the United States in 1876. After going to the great Centennial Exposition in Philadelphia, he came to Boston to meet the famous men of New England, who were gathered at a reception to greet him. When he saw Whittier his face lit up. He took Whittier's arm and drew him aside. They talked until the party was over. A few years earlier Brazil, which depended on slave labor for its cotton and coffee plantations, had passed a law gradually emancipating the slaves. Whittier hoped that the country would soon go the whole way to freedom.

After *Among the Hills* Whittier's next book was *The Pennsylvania Pilgrim and Other Poems.* The pilgrim of the title poem was Francis Daniel Pastorius, the German Quaker who came to Pennsylvania following William Penn and organized in 1688 the first public protest against slavery in the world. Whittier's descriptions of the Pennsylvania farms and woods was as vivid and exact as were his descriptions of his own land along the Merrimack. In this long poem, which he himself thought was better than *Snow-Bound,* he shows his knowledge of the mystics and the great philosophers as well as the history of Pennsylvania, and in it he drew one of his most sensitive pictures of the Quaker meeting at its best.

Lowly before the Unseen Presence knelt
Each waiting heart, till haply some one felt
On his moved lips the seal of silence melt

Or without spoken words, low breathings stole
Of a diviner life from soul to soul
Baptizing in one tender thought the whole.

Besides the four books of poems that he wrote during the decade after *Among the Hills,* Whittier also edited, with Lucy Larcom, three anthologies for children: *Child Life,* a collection of poems; *Child Life in Prose;* and *Songs of Three Centuries,* from which the peace lovers excluded all war poems except "The Battle Hymn of the Republic." Lucy Larcom had given up school-teaching for editing; she was editor of a new magazine for children called *Our Young Folks,* to which Whittier contributed poems from time to time.

The Amesbury house had a succession of pets, of which the dearest was Charlie, a gray parrot with a scarlet tail. They got him while Mrs. Whittier was still living, and she had been very fond of him. He liked to perch on Whittier's chair at mealtime and accept tidbits from the table. He liked also to climb to the roof of the house and shout "Whoa!" at passing horses, which would then obediently stop, to their drivers' annoyance. At first he had had the profane vocabulary that parrots are commonly supposed to possess, but gradually under Quaker influence his language improved. One Sunday morning, though, he disgraced them all by climbing to the chimney top and from there swearing at church-goers passing by. His death came as a result of perching on the chimney and falling down into it. Whittier wrote to Lucy Larcom, "He was an old friend; dear Lizzie liked him. And he was the heartiest, jolliest, pleasantest old fellow I ever saw."

Charlie was succeeded by a rooster, which also perched on Whittier's shoulder. When his niece Lizzie slept late, Whittier would put the rooster on the top of her door to awaken her with his crowing. There were also a gray squirrel, which climbed into Whittier's pocket for nuts and sometimes upset the papers on his desk, and a dog named Charles Dickens.

Whittier never owned a carriage horse, though he contributed ten dollars when a subscription was got up to buy a horse and carriage for Walt Whitman. But sometimes he would hire one to take a friend for a drive. Once when he was driving Lucy Larcom, the horse was fresh and frisky. Lucy, inclined to be dreamy, talked on, not noticing Whittier's struggles with the horse, about her ideas of the life after death, until Whittier exclaimed, "Lucy! If thee doesn't stop talking till I get this horse in hand, thee'll be in heaven before thee wants to!"

After his niece married in April 1876 and went to live in Portland, Maine, there was an empty place in the house and in Whittier's life. His cousins, Joseph and Gertrude Cartland, spent most of that year with him before they bought a house in New-buryport. It was the house once lived in by Harriet Livermore, the "not unfeared, half-welcome guest" of *Snow-Bound,* and Whittier often visited them there.

But the house where for the rest of his life he spent part of each year was Oak Knoll in Danvers. This was the home of three sisters, Mrs. Henry Woodman, Miss Caroline Cartland Johnson, and Miss May Johnson, who were cousins of Whittier's and nieces of Joseph Cartland. Mrs. Woodman had an adopted daughter, Phoebe, a young girl who became a devoted friend of Whittier's. She helped him answer his many letters when he was at Oak Knoll, and when he was away from there he wrote often to her. Caroline Cartland Johnson, who had a school in Boston, had been offered the presidency of Wellesley College. Moses Cartland said of her, "There was always an intellectual sunshine in her presence."

Oak Knoll was an estate of some sixty acres, with many beautiful and rare trees, a twenty-acre lawn, an orchard, and flower and vegetable gardens. The large, white-columned house, in which Whittier had a bedroom and a study, was set upon a hill facing a grassy knoll with an oak and a chestnut tree. No doubt an added attraction for the legend-loving Whittier was the fact that in the seventeenth century it had been the home of Ann Putnam, reputed to be a witch, who entertained her young witch friends there, and of the Reverend George Burroughs, who came to a bad end as a wizard.

When Whittier reached the age of seventy, the whole country rose up to celebrate his birthday with affection and enthusiasm. Letters and presents poured in, the newspapers were full of tributes. A magazine, the *Literary World,* devoted a whole issue to him, with poems and articles about him by all the well-known writers of the country. There was even a picture of Oak Knoll.

Most important was a great dinner given in his honor by the *Atlantic Monthly.* When it was first planned, he resisted the idea. "They are wanting to make a fuss over my birthday on the

Oak Knoll

17th," he wrote to Lizzie. "I think I have put a stop to it." But he had not. More than sixty notables gathered at the Hotel Brunswick in Boston to do him honor.

Emerson, Longfellow, Holmes, and a new young writer from the West, Mark Twain, sat at the head table with him. When Whittier was introduced, all the guests stood up and cheered. Whittier uttered a few words of thanks and then asked Longfellow to read the modest and grateful poem, "Response," which he had written for the occasion. Emerson read Whittier's poem, "Ichabod," and Oliver Wendell Holmes read a poem of his own, in which he called Whittier "the wood-thrush of Essex," the most felicitous of all the many tributes paid him.

Afterwards he wrote characteristically to a friend, "Overpraise pains like blame."

16. Love to
All the World

Most of the hymns by Whittier that are sung today in churches of all denominations were not written as hymns to be sung. They are poems or parts of poems which have been set to music and sometimes changed a little to suit the theology of the church publishing the hymnal. From his long poem, "Our Master," for instance, three hymns have been taken and two from "The Eternal Goodness." Others come from "The Vision of Eckhard," "The Shadow and the Light," and others.

Probably the most widely sung and best loved hymn is the one beginning "Dear Lord and Father of Mankind." This consists of five or six stanzas of a seventeen-stanza poem called "The Brewing of Soma." Soma was a drink made from the juice of a plant of the milkweed family, used in India a thousand or more years before Christ to induce a mystical experience—as some people hope to have a mystical experience today from taking LSD. Whittier described the ritual of the brewing of the drink, "in the childhood of the world," and the "sacred madness" and "drunken joy" that followed. He referred also to other foolish things done in the name of religion down through the centuries, and then came the stanzas of the hymn, beginning,

Dear Lord and Father of mankind,
  Forgive our foolish ways,
Reclothe us in our rightful mind,
In purer lives Thy service find,
  In deeper reverence praise!

The test of a religion was the goodness of the people who followed it, not the excellence of their belief. He had no use for "creeds of iron and lives of ease." Belief, to be sound, must issue in helpful action, in love and truth. The really religious man, to Whittier, was the one

Who counts his brother's welfare
  As sacred as his own.

Salvation, to him, was "salvation from our selfishness." Ritual and ceremony were to him unnecessary and distracting; in silence the Inward Light shone in each heart, and insights came that were to be carried out in service to other people.

As a Quaker, he was never exclusive. He had more non-Quaker friends than Quaker. As a Christian, he did not despise other religions. All men in his view were brothers, all received in some measure the Light Within.

O brother man, fold to thy heart thy brother—
  Where pity dwells the peace of God is there,
To worship rightly is to love each other,
  Each smile a hymn, each kindly deed a prayer.

All souls that struggle and aspire,
  All hearts of prayer by Thee are lit.

As he grew older he saw death come to many of his friends and knew that inevitably it would come to him. He thought much about it. Many people wrote to ask him if he believed in an afterlife. He could not know, he answered them; no one could know; but he could trust. When he was seventy-six he wrote a poem, "At Last," which he thought best expressed how he felt about the question. He wanted no gates of pearl or streets of gold; he asked only for God's presence—and expressed the hope that familiar hands would beckon him to "some humble door among Thy many mansions."

> *There, from the music round me stealing*
> *I fain would learn the new and holy song,*
> *And find at last beneath Thy trees of healing*
> *The life for which I long.*

No other American poet has expressed religious insights in the gentle, acceptable, and beautiful way that John Greenleaf Whittier has. Among the English poets, Milton is far grander, John Donne is a greater poet and a finer theologian, Henry Vaughan and George Herbert wrote more exquisite and distinguished lyrics. But a cultivated taste for poetry is necessary if one is really to understand and enjoy them. Whittier wrote so that any loving, seeking, or grieving soul could understand and be comforted and strengthened.

Whittier spent the years between his seventieth birthday and his death at eighty-four partly at Oak Knoll, partly in Amesbury, where his friends Judge and Mrs. Cate, who occupied his house, kept a room always ready for him, and partly in the New Hampshire hills. Wherever he went he was surrounded by friends. Those two friends of his youth, Harriet Minot, now Mrs. Pitman, and Elizabeth Neall, now Mrs. Gay, wrote to him regularly. His old doctor friend, Henry L. Bowditch, lived almost as long as he did. Celia Thaxter, Lydia Maria Child, Gail Hamilton, Elizabeth Stuart Phelps wrote often and came to see him. There was also a new friend, a young woman writer forty-two years younger than he, who became like a daughter to him.

Sarah Orne Jewett, whose best book, *The Country of the Pointed Firs,* an American classic, was not to be written till after Whittier's death, published in 1876 a collection of sketches of Maine life that Whittier liked very much. He wrote to her about it, and so their friendship began. She was born and grew up in the village of South Berwick, Maine, not far from Portsmouth, and she was a great friend of Annie Fields. After James Fields's death Sarah Orne Jewett spent most of her winters in Boston with Mrs. Fields. They gave very elegant literary parties in the second-story drawing room overlooking the Charles River, but Whittier, who did not like crowds, never came to these. Instead, when he was in Boston, he would come to breakfast with them, and they would linger long at the table, talking. Sometimes Sarah and Annie joined Whittier at Holderness or Center Harbor in the summer. Sometimes they came to Amesbury or Oak Knoll to see him. Because he signed his letters to Sarah "Truly thy friend" and the Quaker *thee* and *thy* seemed to her quaint, she always referred to him when she was writing to Annie Fields, as "thy friend." Several letters from her to Annie describe her visits to Whittier, but one will give the flavor of them all.

She had gone to Amesbury at teatime and stayed till 10 P.M. "He was even more affectionate and dear than usual," she wrote, "and seemed uncommonly well, though he had had neuralgia all day. . . . But oh how rich we are with 'thy friend' for a friend. He looked really stout for him and his face was so full of youth and pleasure and eagerness of interest, as we talked, that it was good only to see him. The LLD [Harvard had recently given him an honorary doctorate of laws] had evidently given him pleasure, though he was quite shy about it. He was full of politics but we also touched upon Wallace and my old grand-uncle. . . . and he told a string of his delicious old country stories."

Though the Civil War was long over and slavery abolished, he saw as most other people did not that the Negroes were still not wholly free. They labored under the burden of prejudice and poverty and lack of education. In the South they were deprived of the vote.

In 1879 the Jubilee Singers of Fisk University made a successful tour of Europe, singing their spirituals before seven kings and emperors, but on their return they were driven out of an American hotel at midnight because of their color. They visited Whittier in Amesbury and sang for him alone in his garden room. He listened with tears in his eyes; afterward he wrote a poem to them:

Voices of a ransomed race, sing on
Till Freedom's every right is won,
And slavery's every wrong undone!

He still studied the character of political leaders and wrote letters about candidates to the newspapers. Justice for women became a concern of his—not a new one, for in 1839 he had written to Elizabeth Neall, "I go the whole length as regards the rights of women—though," he admitted, "I sometimes joke a little about it." But in all seriousness he had written to a convention on woman suffrage held in Boston in 1869:

> I am more than willing to welcome women to the same rights which I enjoy. . . . On the other hand I do not see that the exercise of the ballot by woman will prove a remedy for all the ills of which she justly complains. It is her right as truly as mine and when she asks for it, it is something less than manhood to withhold it. But unsupported by a more practical education, higher aims and a deeper sense of the responsibilities of life and duty, it is not likely to prove a blessing in her hands any more than in man's.

In 1881 he wrote to the board of trustees of Brown University, of which he was a member, urging that the university open its doors to women.

His brother Frank died in February 1882, and Longfellow the following month. His brother, he said, had been a kind, unselfish man who had had a hard life. Longfellow had been his friend for many years. He missed them both. "It seems as if I could never write again," he wrote to Thomas Bailey Aldrich, now the editor of the *Atlantic Monthly*. "A feeling of unutterable sadness and loneliness oppresses me."

But by the following summer, he was writing again. He had a love of life and of nature that was never quenched. Though some friends died, he still had many to love, and love became more and more the climate of his life. "I enjoy life; it is a pleasant thing to behold the sun. I love nature in her varied aspects and as I grow older I find more to love in my fellow creatures and more to pity," he wrote to one friend. And to another, "I realize more and more that fame and notoriety can avail little in our situation; that love is the one essential thing, always welcome, outliving time and change and going with us into the unguessed possibilities of death."

As the older poets disappeared, Oliver Wendell Holmes and Whittier drew closer together. "We are more than literary friends," Whittier said, "we *love* each other." A young woman novelist who was at lunch one day with both of them recorded her delight in their brilliant and witty conversation. Holmes, who had been for years on the faculty of the Harvard Medical School, was also a poet and an essayist, best known for his poems "The Constitution" and "The Wonderful One-Hoss Shay" and for his book of essays, *The Autocrat of the Breakfast-Table*. He wrote to Whittier, thanking him for the gift of a volume of his poems: "Who has preached the gospel of love to such a mighty congregation as you have preached it?"

John Greenleaf Whittier. Photograph by Mathew Brady

When he was eighty-one Whittier prepared a definitive edition of his work, four volumes of poetry and three of prose. He was critical about his own work. He wrote to Annie Fields that he would like to drown many of his poems "like so many unlikely kittens, but my publishers say there is no getting rid of them. They have more than nine lives." Some of them he changed here and there to improve the grammar or the rhymes.

This was almost his last work. He wrote a few more poems, which he had privately printed in a little volume called *At Sundown*. He dedicated it to Oliver Wendell Holmes. "I have been ill all summer, but the world is still fair to me; my friends are very dear to me. I love and am loved."

Birthdays were always a time for his friends to express to him their continuing affection and admiration. He especially appreciated the letters which came from Black students in the South. Sometimes they sent him barrels of pitch pine for kindling his fire. One of the letters he liked best came from a little girl who had made her way out of the double prison of blindness and deafness. Helen Keller was at the Perkins School for the Blind and she wrote him that she and her friends were going to celebrate his birthday by reading his poems. He wrote back thanking her, saying, "I do not wonder that thee thinks eighty-three years a long time, but to me it seems but a very little while since I was a boy no older than thee, playing on the old farm at Haverhill."

His eighty-fourth birthday he spent with Joseph and Gertrude Cartland in their house at Newburyport. Between five and six hundred people came to see him and two thousand wrote letters. The Whittier Club of Haverhill arrived with eighty-four pink rosebuds. Three of his schoolmates from the Haverhill Academy came. Seven hundred Vassar students sent a telegram. But "the best thing," he wrote to Annie Fields, "was to meet thee and our dear Sarah on the stairs, and the worst was that you went away so soon."

The following summer he did not go to Center Harbor or to Intervale, but visited instead his old friend and distant cousin, Sarah A. Gove in Hampton Falls, only seven miles from Amesbury, in the old house called Elmfield where he had gone as a child with his mother to stay. From the upstairs balcony on which his room opened he could see the Hampton meadows and the ocean with its sails. Joseph and Gertrude Cartland were there too and his niece Lizzie Pickard, and young people came to sit on the lawn with him.

While he was there he suffered a severe stroke. His friends took loving care of him during the four days that he lived. Again and again during that time he said, "Love—love to all the world." His long life ended on September 7, 1892, a little more than three months before his eighty-fifth birthday.

It had covered almost all of the nineteenth century. Through all of it he had stood for freedom and for love. He had given sound advice to politicians. He had helped to bring about the freeing of the slaves. He had awakened interest in the old tales and legends of New England. He had written poems that explained America to itself during years of great change and of large influxes of new people into the country. He had written of a religion so universal that all denominations could sing his hymns. He had been greatly loved as a poet and as a man.

His immense popularity was to fade away in the new century, which turned from Longfellow and Lowell as well as from Whittier. But some of his poems still stand today as a true and beautiful expression of the American spirit, and he still points us on toward respect for the humanity of all men that is the necessary accompaniment of freedom.

A Partial Bibliography

Currier, Thomas Franklin, ed. *Elizabeth Lloyd and the Whittiers. A Budget of Letters*. Cambridge: Harvard University Press, 1939.

Denervaud, Marie V., ed. *Whittier's Unknown Romance*. Boston: Houghton Mifflin, 1922.

Pickard, John B. *John Greenleaf Whittier: An Introduction and Interpretation*. New York: Holt, Rinehart and Winston, 1961.

Pickard, Samuel T. *Life and Letters of John Greenleaf Whittier*. 2 vols. Boston: Houghton Mifflin, 1894.

Pollard, John C. *John Greenleaf Whittier, Friend of Man*. Boston: Houghton Mifflin, 1949.

Wagenknecht, Edward. *John Greenleaf Whittier: A Portrait in Paradox*. New York: Oxford University Press, 1967.

Warren, Robert Penn. *John Greenleaf Whittier's Poetry: An Appraisal and a Selection*. Minneapolis: University of Minnesota Press, 1971.

Whittier, John Greenleaf. *Complete Poetical and Prose Works*. 7 vols. Boston: Houghton Mifflin, 1888.

Index